MW00931411

Copyright Statement

Notice of Liability

This book was written by Neil Perlin, Hyper/Word Services (www.hyperword.com). Send all suggestions or corrections to nperlin@nperlin.cnc.net

Dedication

Thanks to Bill, Bruce, and TJ at GTAT in Merrimack, NH where I taught a Flare 8 class in early 2012. Your questions about the float feature motivated me to finally write this book, the idea for which had been germinating for years as I made note of the questions that people had in Flare classes or that just came in over the transom.

Thanks to the folks in tech support over the years who've clarified several confusing areas. You know who you are and it's great to have you all around as a backstop.

And, as always, heartfelt thanks to Connie, whose courage, openness to new things, and adaptability to what looks to outsiders like total chaos makes this book and this life possible.

Table of Contents

Copyright Statement **1**

Notice of Liability 1

Dedication..**2**

Table of Contents...**3**

Introduction **8**

Float Property for Graphic Position Control.......**10**

Float Options...14

Clear 15

Vertical Alignment...16

Float Use Through Styles.......................................16

Differences Between Inline and Style-Based Applications of Floats...20

DOCTYPE...**25**

Mark of the Web...**27**

Pseudo Code vs. Full Code Views **29**

Pseudo Code View for Flare 8, 9, and 10.............29

Full Code View in Flare 8 30

Full Code View in Flare 9 32

Accessing Full Code View...............................32

Simultaneous View Display and Orientation.....34

Syntax Coloring 37

Full Code View in Flare 10 39

HTML 5 Output **41**

Public-Facing Content..41

Hybrid Apps..43

1st Heading and Title Options When Creating a New Topic **46**

Topic Templates – Creating and Adding to the Flare Interface..**51**

Toggler Links **57**

Master Pages vs. Page Layouts..............................**64**

Master Pages 64

Page Layouts 67

Linked vs Unlinked Table of Contents Headings 71

Relative vs Absolute Units of Measure for Styles 76

Unbind 79

Hyperlinks vs. Cross-References............................80

Format Cross-References to Show Page Numbers in Printed Output..85

Manually Update Cross-References.....................88

How to Create and Use Mediums........................89

How to Delete Mediums 96

Change the Display of Style Properties on the Stylesheet Editor 98

How Flare's Styles Pane Differs From Other HATs and Word 103

Local Formatting and the Styles Pane.................105

List Styles - Applying 109

Numbered List "Continuation" Style.................113

Adding a "Real" ToC and Index to PDF Output118

In Flare 10 - Auto-Generated Print Proxies 124

Change the Width of the Index Marker Field ...127

Word Import – Effect of Source Styles Options on Stylesheet Tab **129**

Word Import – Split Long Topics Option on Options Tab **132**

Word Import – Avoid Creating Empty Topics Option on Options Tab **135**

Word Import – Auto-Reimport Option on Options Tab **139**

Context-Sensitive Help **142**

The Formal Road to CSH 144

The Shortcut to CSH 145

WebHelp AIR **150**

Master Project (Flare Project Import) Considerations **156**

Apply One or More CSSs to a Project **160**

Popups – Topic vs. Text – Design Considerations 163

Slideshows **166**

Converting "Special" links When Outputting to Print **172**

Glossary Term Conversion Options on Target Editor's Glossary Tab **174**

Glossary – Text vs Linked Definitions..............**182**

Mobile Outputs – ePub, WebHelp, WebHelp Mobile, HTML5...**188**

Conditional Build Tags **195**

Some Examples of Conditionality....................195

Working With Conditional Build Tags 197

The Logic of Conditionality 197

Basic and Advanced Build Tagging....................199

Responsive Design and the "Un-Desktop"........**205**

What Is Responsive Design?..............................205

Relative Formatting 210

Fluid Grids 211

Media Queries...212

Responsive Design in Flare...............................213

Summary of Responsive Design 219

Equation Editor **220**

Index **224**

Introduction

MadCap Software's Flare is one of the most powerful, feature-rich, and forward-looking HATs (help authoring tools) on the market. This also causes some problems...

Flare has many features that are so advanced that their purpose and concept are unfamiliar to many users, especially those who are self-taught. Consider the Mark of the Web (MOTW) option on the Target Editor's Advanced tab – a simple, click-box option but what does it do? Why and when should you use it? Or the DOCTYPE option on the Target Editor's Advanced tab – another simple, click-box option, but what does it do? When to use it?

Not all the advanced or unusual features are in the Target Editor. For example, the New Topic dialog box offers two fields labeled "1st Heading" and "Title" that seem to be the same thing. They're not, but what's the difference? The TOC Editor lets you create linked or unlinked TOC headings; the choice affects how some elements of a master page function in the output. What's the equation editor? What's responsive design? What's the difference between the Boolean AND and OR in a conditional build expression? And so on...

This book is based on nine years of consulting and training as a MadCap-certified Flare trainer and consultant, and another twenty two working with online help systems before Flare appeared. The questions that I got from clients and in training classes pointed toward the features that I cover in the book. There's no order to the material, so scan the table of contents to see what looks interesting and check the index.

The book covers features in Flare 8 and 9 as well as the current version, 10. In many cases, the features are identical or similar in both versions. In a few cases, they differ widely and the discussion goes into detail about the differences.

The list of advanced and unfamiliar features will no doubt expand as MadCap releases new versions of Flare. Until then, feel free to suggest topics that I should add to later releases of the book - email me at nperlin@nperlin.cnc.net. And with that, let's go.

Float Property for Graphic Position Control

Applies to versions 8, 9 and 10.

Flare has supported the float property since v.6, but few authors use it because its purpose and use aren't clear. According to the W3C (WorldWide Web Consortium), "…float… specifies whether or not a box (an element) should float." (http://www.w3schools.com/cssref/ pr_class_float.asp). This is accurate but not very helpful.

The float property lets you control the position of graphics on the screen by themselves or in conjunction with text or other graphics or elements. For example, assume that you want to use a standard icon for Notes in your help. You probably create a two-column, one-row table and insert the icon in the left column and the text in the right column.

We've used this familiar tables-as-graphic-positioning-tool approach for years. The problem is that this approach uses tables for layout control, not for tabular information. In order words, it uses tables for a task for which they're not intended and which might backfire in the future.

If you shouldn't position graphics using tables, then how should you do it? The answer is float. Float can get very complex, so a full explanation is beyond the scope of this book. There are also some inconsistencies in how Flare implements the float feature. Nevertheless, it is worth understanding so this section introduces the use of float and some of its details and offers references for research on your own. Look for a more detailed discussion in a later version of this book.

So how does float work?

Float lets you specify programmatically where a graphic should appear by itself or in relation to text or other screen elements, such as the Note example mentioned a few paragraphs above. For example, let's say you have the image and text shown below and want the image on the left and the text on the right.

These are my 10 and 12" mirrors. The 10" is ground to 1/5000" and ready for polishing. The 12" is just at the beginning, grinding with 1/40" grit, with 9/1000" out of 25/1000" taken off so far.

Right-click on the graphic, select Edit Image, and select the Position tab when the Edit Image dialog box opens. You'll see three sets of options – Float, Clear, and Vertical Alignment.

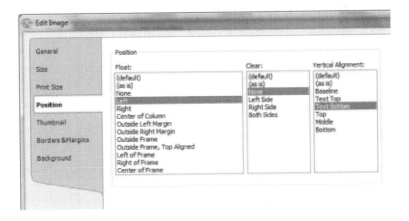

For a simple example, here's the result if you select Right from the Float group.

These are my 10 and 12" mirrors. The 10" is ground to 1/5000" and ready for polishing. The 12" is just at the beginning, grinding with 1/40" grit, with 9/1000" out of 25/1000" taken off so far.]

Oops. We should have positioned (floated) the graphic to the left of the text. Simply select Left from the Float group. Here's the result.

These are my 10 and 12" mirrors. The 10" is ground to 1/5000" and ready for polishing. The 12" is just at the beginning, grinding with 1/40" grit, with 9/1000" out of 25/1000" taken off so far.

Better, but it needs more space between the image and text. Right-click on the graphic, select Edit Image, select the Borders & Margins tab on the Edit Image dialog box, and change the Right margin from 0px to 20px, for example. Here's the result.

These are my 10 and 12" mirrors. The 10" is ground to 1/5000" and ready for polishing. The 12" is just at the beginning, grinding with 1/40" grit, with 9/1000" out of 25/1000" taken off so far.

If we add 20px of Right padding, here's the result.

These are my 10 and 12" mirrors. The 10" is ground to 1/5000" and ready for polishing. The 12" is just at the beginning, grinding with 1/40" grit, with 9/1000" out of 25/1000" taken off so far.

Padding adds space between the image and the right border of the box that contains it, in addition to the space between the box and the text. To make this easier to see, let's recreate the two images above but with a border. First with a Right margin of 20 but the Right padding of 0.

These are my 10 and 12" mirrors. The 10" is ground to 1/5000" and ready for polishing. The 12" is just at the beginning, grinding with 1/40" grit, with 9/1000" out of 25/1000" taken off so far.]

There's a border around the graphic, although it's hard to see. Here's the image again but with the Right padding set to 20. This pushes the border out to the right by 20px.

These are my 10 and 12" mirrors. The 10" is ground to 1/5000" and ready for polishing. The 12" is just at the beginning, grinding with 1/40" grit, with 9/1000" out of 25/1000" taken off so far.

To recap, adjusting the padding adjusts the space between the image and the "box" that contains the image – e.g. it adjusts the space inside the box. Adjusting the margin adjusts the space outside the box.

Let's review the Float, Clear, and Vertical Alignment properties.

Float Options

The Float property lets you specify where to position the graphic by itself or in relation to other elements. The options are:

- None – Displays the graphic where it occurs in the text, with no float. This is the default.
- Left – Floats the graphic to the left of the text, allowing text to the right of the graphic.
- Right – Floats the graphic to the right of the text, allowing text to the left of the graphic.
- Center of Column – Positions the image in the center of the column on the page.
- Outside Left Margin – Positions the image beyond the left margin of the topic text.
- Outside Right Margin – Positions the image beyond the right margin of the topic text.

- Outside Frame – Positions the image outside of the page frame.
- Outside Frame, Top Aligned – Positions the image outside of the page frame, as well as aligning it with the top of the frame.
- Left of Frame – Positions the image to the left of the page frame.
- Right of Frame – Positions the image to the right of the page frame.
- Center of Frame – Positions the image both vertically and horizontally in the middle of the page frame.

(The descriptions of the last eight items are from the Flare WebHelp at webhelp.madcapsoftware.com. For more information, see http://www.w3.org/wiki/Floats_and_clearing and at "Everything You Never Knew About CSS Floats" by Joshua Johnson at design shack, http://designshack.net/articles/css/everything-you-never-knew-about-css-floats/)

Clear

The Clear property lets you specify that other elements cannot appear on certain sides of a floated graphic. An element next to a graphic will be forced down below the graphic. The options are:

- None – Allows floating elements on both sides. The default.
- Left Side – Doesn't allow floating elements on the left side.

- Right Side – Doesn't allow floating elements on the right side.
- Both Sides – Doesn't allow floating elements on either side.

Vertical Alignment

The Vertical Alignment property lets you set an element's vertical alignment. This property has six options – baseline, text top and bottom, and top, middle, and bottom.

Float Use Through Styles

The process discussed so far – right-click on the graphic to float, select Edit Image, select the Positioning and Borders & Margins tabs on the Edit Image dialog box – is inline formatting. You can work this way if you want to format every graphic individually. However, if you want to apply a standard set of properties to all graphics, or groups of graphics, you'll want to apply the float properties using styles instead. Flare's Stylesheet Editor offers the float properties described above but in different, somewhat inconsistent ways. They all work, but you'll have to be alert to the differences. I'll describe them below.

Float is a property of the img tag. Use it by defining its properties for the img tag if you want to assign the float property to all your graphics, or by creating a sub-class of img and assigning the float properties to that sub-class if you want to be able to assign different float properties to different groups of graphics. Let's take a look at using the latter approach.

First create the sub-class by either:

- Right-clicking on the img style in the Stylesheet Editor, selecting Add Class, and naming the class in the New Style dialog box, or
- Clicking on the img style in the Stylesheet Editor, clicking the Add Class button on the Stylesheet Editor toolbar, and naming the class in the New Style dialog box.

The image below shows a sub-class called image_float that displays below img. (image_float is a child style of img.) The image also shows that the Float property, shown in the Box group in the Properties list on the right side of the screen, is set to Right.

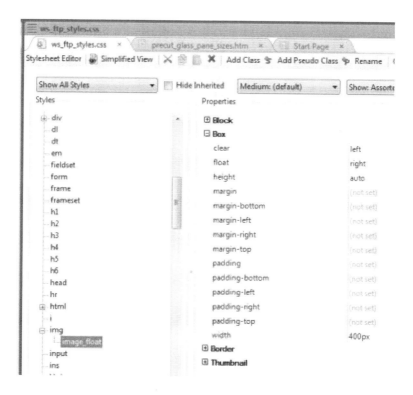

You can also set the margins, padding, and other properties, like any other style.

You then assign the image_float style to your graphics. To do so, go to a topic that contains a graphic, right-click on the graphic and click on Style Class at the bottom of the dropdown menu. You'll see a list of available sub-classes for the class of the element on which you clicked. (Here, because you right-clicked on an element that has an img tag, you'll see the sub-classes of img, in this case image_float. See the image below.)

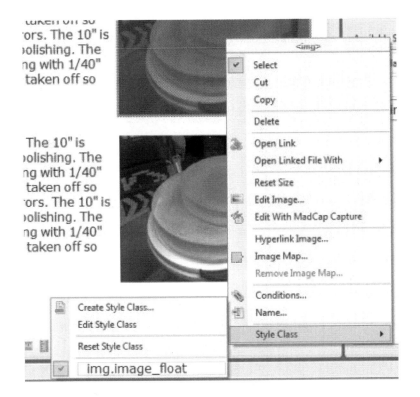

Clicking on img.image_float applies that style, which includes the float settings, to the image. You do this for each image to which you wanted to apply the same float and other properties.

What's the result? In the previous image, the float is set to Right and the image floats to the right of the text. Change the float to Left and the effect is as shown below.

These are my 10 and 12" mirrors. The 10" is ground to 1/5000" and ready for polishing. The 12" is just at the beginning, grinding with 1/40" grit, with 9/1000" out of 25/1000" taken off so far. These are my 10 and 12" mirrors. The 10" is ground to 1/5000" and ready for polishing. The 12" is just at the beginning, grinding with 1/40" grit, with 9/1000" out of 25/1000" taken off so far.

These are my 10 and 12" mirrors. The 10" is ground to 1/5000" and ready for polishing. The 12" is just at the beginning, grinding with 1/40" grit, with 9/1000" out of 25/1000" taken off so far. These are my 10 and 12" mirrors. The 10" is ground to 1/5000" and ready for polishing. The 12" is just at the beginning, grinding with 1/40" grit, with 9/1000" out of 25/1000" taken off so far.

As usual, changing the style changed every element to which the style was assigned, here the two graphics. The blocks of text are too close to their respective graphics but that's easy to fix by widening the right margin in the style.

Differences Between Inline and Style-Based Applications of Floats

Applying the float property via styles offers the consistency you'd get with any style. However, be aware of some inconsistencies in how Flare's Stylesheet Editor currently handles float.

In the Stylesheet Editor's Simplified View, you access the float options by clicking the Properties icon to the left of the B icon on the Stylesheet Editor toolbar, show below.

This opens the Properties dialog box whose Position tab, shown below, has the same Float, Clear, and Vertical Alignment options you saw in the Edit Image dialog box (and a few extra ones).

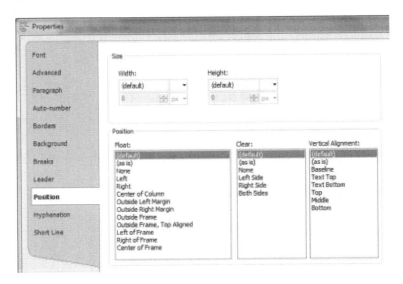

All the options are on one tab, just as they are in the Edit Image dialog box described earlier. However, if you're in the Stylesheet Editor's Advanced View, the options are distributed among other property groups. For example, the Vertical Alignment options are listed on the pulldown of the Vertical Alignment settings dialog box, as shown below, and have two additional options.

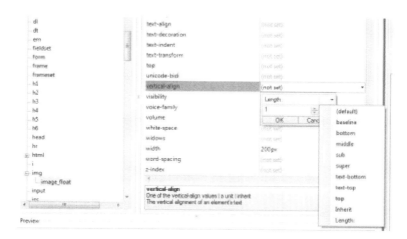

In other words, the features are available in different places in different Stylesheet Editor views.

The display may also be inconsistent depending on the browser, browser version, and even browser window size. For example, there seems to be a line space between the two graphics below.

These are my 10 and 12" mirrors. The 10" is ground to 1/5000" and ready for polishing. The 12" is just at the beginning, grinding with 1/40" grit, with 9/1000" out of 25/1000" taken off so far. These are my 10 and 12" mirrors. The 10" is ground to 1/5000" and ready for polishing. The 12" is just at the beginning, grinding with 1/40" grit, with 9/1000" out of 25/1000" taken off so far.

These are my 10 and 12" mirrors. The 10" is ground to 1/5000" and ready for polishing. The 12" is just at the beginning, grinding with 1/40" grit, with 9/1000" out of 25/1000" taken off so far. These are my 10 and 12" mirrors. The 10" is ground to 1/5000" and ready for polishing. The 12" is just at the beginning, grinding with 1/40" grit, with 9/1000" out of 25/1000" taken off so far.

When you preview this topic or generate and view the output in IE9 and resize the browser window to less than full screen, here's what you'll see…

These are my 10 and 12" mirrors. The 10" is ground to 1/5000" and ready for polishing. The 12" is just at the beginning, grinding with 1/40" grit, with 9/1000" out of 25/1000" taken off so far. These are my 10 and 12" mirrors. The 10" is ground to 1/5000" and ready for polishing. The 12" is just at the beginning, grinding with 1/40" grit, with 9/1000" out of 25/1000" taken off so far.

These are my 10 and 12" mirrors. The 10" is ground to 1/5000" and ready for polishing. The 12" is just at the beginning, grinding with 1/40" grit, with 9/1000" out of 25/1000" taken off so far.

The line space is still there. But when you preview this topic or generate and view the output in IE9 in a full-size browser window, here's what you'll see…

These are my 10 and 12" mirrors. The 10" is gi
just at the beginning, grinding with 1/40" grit,
These are my 10 and 12" mirrors. The 10" is gi
just at the beginning, grinding with 1/40" grit,

These are my 10 and 12" mirrors. The 10" is gi
just at the beginning, grinding with 1/40" grit,
These are my 10 and 12" mirrors. The 10" is gi
just at the beginning, grinding with 1/40" grit,

The line space is gone, the two graphics are run together, and the two text paragraphs are run together on the first graphic.

In summary, the float feature offers a lot of power and appears to be the way to position graphics going forward. However, the inconsistencies between the Simplified and Advanced Stylesheet Editor views in Flare and the "issue" with the Vertical Alignment options and browser inconsistencies suggest that you start to get acquainted with this feature but keep its use very simple for the present.

DOCTYPE

Applies to versions 8, 9, and 10.

This option, on the Advanced tab of the Target Editor for HTML Help output and the WebHelp-based outputs other than WebHelp Mobile, may call for some strategic thought. Basically, selecting this option inserts one additional line of code in your topics, the DOCTYPE entry shown on line 2 in the image below.

If you enable the DOCTYPE feature to add the code to your topics, modern browsers display the topics in "strict" or "standards" mode. If you disable the feature, modern browsers display your topics in "quirks" mode. What does this mean?

Modern browsers increasingly enforce correct code syntax; older browsers are less rigid but those less rigid rules are still available for use. "Strict/standards" mode tells a browser to use the new, rigid rules on your material. Quirks mode tells the browser to use the old, looser rules. How do you decide which mode to use and what's the effect?

A rule of thumb is that if your topics use style tags like floats that don't display correctly, use the DOCTYPE option. If you're not having these problems, then don't bother using the option. It sounds like a simple decision.

But the decision also depends on the browsers your users have now and their browser update trends. Enabling the option prepares your topics to run on modern browsers but may affect their display on older browsers, with the results depending on the browser and version. So not using the DOCTYPE seems to play it safe.

However, the http://hsivonen.iki.fi site has an impassioned plea in favor of using DOCTYPE and against quirks mode – the basic point being to not design for the past. The problem is that while past platforms like IE6 may be officially dead, many of your users may still use them and you don't want to cut off those users. It's a strategic issue and a good illustration of the decisions that your programmers have to make. Talk to them about this.

Mark of the Web

Applies to versions 8, 9, and 10.

When Internet Explorer users open a help topic (an HTM file) on their local PC, they'll see a warning at the bottom of the screen that looks like the one below on Windows 7, or a variant on XP or Vista.

Users *must* click the button to allow the display of blocked content before the topic will display in full. It's a Windows security feature that has nothing to do with viewing help topics but whose secondary effect is to add an extra step before users can see the topic.

You can turn off this security feature as a favor to your users by selecting the Insert Mark of the Web option on the Advanced tab of the Target Editor for WebHelp and HTML5. The help will then open immediately, without the blocked content bar. So selecting this option seems like a good idea. However, there are several reasons for avoiding this feature.

- It applies only to Internet Explorer. If your users don't have Internet Explorer as their default browser, the blocked content isn't an issue.
- It applies only to topics (HTM files/web pages) on users' PCs. It does not apply to topics on a network drive or server. So if your help system only runs from a network drive or server, you don't need Mark of the Web.

- Mark of the Web can also have two side effects for Flare work. First, any links in a topic work when you preview the topic. However, if you enable Mark of the Web, the links don't work in preview mode. It's not an issue if you know and remember that Mark of the Web turns off the link preview, but it's easy to forget and wonder why your link preview suddenly broke. Second, if you create links from topics in a project to external files, such as PDFs, those links won't work in the output and there is no error message. This is very disconcerting to users.

In summary, only use Mark of the Web if your help project runs locally under Internet Explorer and doesn't contain external links.

Pseudo Code vs. Full Code Views

Applies to versions 8, 9, and 10 with differences between the versions in full code view.

Pseudo Code View for Flare 8, 9, and 10

When you click the pulldown on the Show Tags icon, at the right end of the XML Editor toolbar shown below, it's easy to accidentally click on the icon instead of the pulldown and see your topic's display change dramatically

For example, this topic:

Suddenly looks like this:

```
<html+>
    <head></head>
    <body+>
        <h1+>My Test Topic</h1>
        <p+>Delete this text and replace it with your own content.</p>
        <MadCap:dropDown+>
            <MadCap:dropDownHead+><MadCap:dropDownHotspot+>Dropdown hotspot tex

            </MadCap:dropDownHead>
            <MadCap:dropDownBody+>
                <p+>Dropdown text that displays when the user clicks the hotspot
            </MadCap:dropDownBody>
        </MadCap:dropDown>
    </body>
</html>
```

(The image is enlarged for easier reading, and some text is truncated on the right edge.)

This view shows a summary of the code. MadCap calls it the "pseudo code view". People sometimes read this term as "view of pseudo code" but it really means a "pseudo view of the code".

```
<html+>
    <head></head>
    <body+>
        <h1+>My Test Topic</h1>
        <p+>Delete this text and replace it with your own content.</p>
        <MadCap:dropDown->
    </body>
</html>
```

Authors sometimes mistake pseudo code view as the place to edit the topic code. It's not; it's just a way to view the topic structure. To edit the XHTML code, go to full code view in Flare.

Full Code View in Flare 8

To access full code view in Flare 8, click the Send… file to editor icon at the right end of the topic toolbar, to the right of the Show Tags icon, shown below.

The topic displays in full code view, as shown below.

```
Text Editor
1  <?xml version="1.0" encoding="utf-8"?>
2  <html xmlns:MadCap="http://www.madcapsoftware.com/Schemas/MadCap.xsd" MadCap:ignoredWord
   lastBlockDepth="4" MadCap:lastHeight="154" MadCap:lastWidth="830">
3    <head>
4    </head>
5    <body>
6      <h1>My Test Topic</h1>
7      <p>Delete this text and replace it with your own content.</p>
8      <MadCap:dropDown>
9        <MadCap:dropDownHead>
10         <MadCap:dropDownHotspot style="font-family: Verdana;">Dropdown hotspot t
11         </MadCap:dropDownHead>
12       <MadCap:dropDownBody>
13         <p>Dropdown text that displays when the user clicks the hotspot above.</
14       </MadCap:dropDownBody>
15       </MadCap:dropDown>
16     </body>
17 </html>
```

You can now modify the topic directly in the code.
However, be aware of three things before working in code.

- Flare will ask you to save the XML Editor (WYSIWYG) mode before it opens the topic in code view.
- If you modify the code and then save the topic, Flare will check the syntax of the changes to be sure they're valid. If they're not, you'll have to fix the errors before Flare will let you view the topic in the WYSIWYG XML Editor. In other words, you have to do it right or else you'll have to discard your changes. Don't work in code view unless you know XHTML and back up carefully.
- You can also go to code view by right-clicking a topic in the Content Explorer and selecting Open With > Internal Text Editor. This opens the topic in the same editor you get by clicking the Send to…

icon or the Text Editor tab. It's just another way to get to the code. However, do not select the Open With > Notepad option. You can work in Notepad but this has two drawbacks. First, lines aren't numbered. Second, Flare won't be aware of your changes and you'll have to reimport the changed topic into Flare.

Full Code View in Flare 9

Flare 9 has several significant changes to the code view feature, starting with how to access it.

Accessing Full Code View

To access full code view, click the Text Editor tab on the right edge of the topic window, shown in the highlight in the image below. There are two tabs there, XML Editor and Text Editor. Clicking them switches between WYSIWYG and code views.

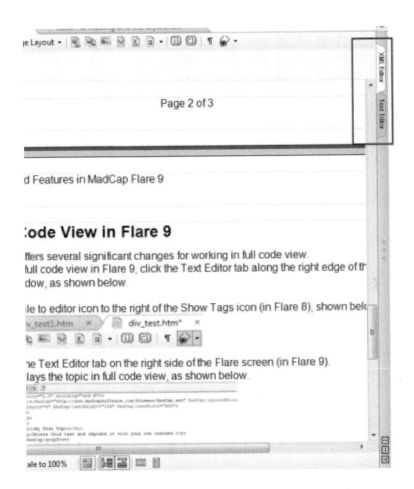

Here's what the same topic looks like in full code view.

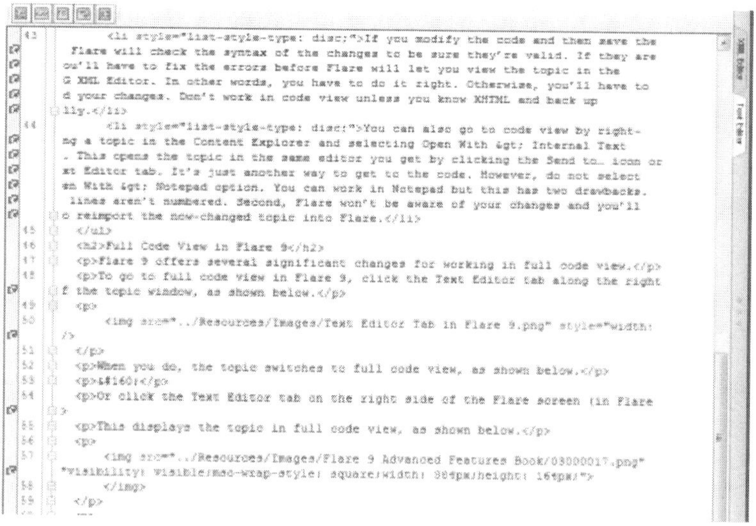

Each view takes up the entire editor working area.

Simultaneous-View Display and Orientation

Sometimes you may want to see both views at once. To do so, click the left-facing arrow icon at the bottom of the bar that contains the XML Editor and Text Editor tabs, shown in the highlight box in the image below. You'll see both views at once in two equally narrow windows, shown below.

You may want to see both views but make one pane wider than the other. To do so, drag the vertical bar below the XML Editor and Text Editor tabs. (Look for three little circles halfway down the bar if you're not sure where to click.) The result might look like this.

The screen examples shown so far have been split vertically, with WYSIWYG view on the left and full code view on the right. You can reverse the two views by clicking the left/right arrows between the XML Editor and Text Editor tabs.

You can also switch from a vertically split screen to a horizontally split one by clicking the appropriate split icon highlighted on the screen above. The screen shot below shows the same topic views in a horizontal split.

Syntax Coloring

Flare displays different components of an XHTML file in different colors to make it easier for you to spot the component to change. The colors are:

- Black - Content.
- Dark red - Style tags.
- Red - Style attributes.
- Blue - Values.

For example, on line 43 of the screen below, the first line in the image, the style tag li is dark red, the attribute name style is red, the attribute value list-style_type... is blue, and the body text of that list item is black.

The toolbar at the upper left corner of the text editor offers various options:

- Turn line numbering on or off. I recommend keeping it on to help you keep track of where you are in a complex file.
- Collapse or expand any sub-entries within a style tag.
- Turn the syntax coloring on or off. I recommend keeping it on to add visual distinction to what's otherwise a blob of text.
- Turn word wrapping on or off. I recommend keeping it on in order to avoid extensive horizontal scrolling.
- Turn the autocomplete feature on or off. This feature makes Flare suggest possible tags based on what you type and the type of document you're editing.

Be aware of three things before working in the code.

- Flare may ask you to save the WYSIWYG mode before it opens the topic in code view. If it does, save.
- If you modify the code and then save the topic, Flare will check the syntax of the changes to be sure they're valid. If they are not, you'll have to fix the errors before Flare will let you save the topic. In other words, you have to do it right. Otherwise, you'll have to discard your changes. Don't work in code view unless you know XHTML and back up carefully.
- You can also go to code view by right-clicking a topic in the Content Explorer and selecting Open With > Internal Text Editor. This opens the topic in the same editor you get by clicking the Send to… icon or the Text Editor tab. It's just another way to get to the code. Do not select the Open With > Notepad option. You can work in Notepad but this has two drawbacks. First, lines aren't numbered. Second, Flare won't be aware of your changes and you'll have to reimport the now-changed topic into Flare.

Full Code View in Flare 10

Full code view in Flare 10 is similar to Flare 9, with some additional enhancements.

- When you're in split view, highlighting text in WYSIWYG view highlights the corresponding content in code view.
- The numbers in the upper right corner of the text editor are the pointer's character and line position.

For example, 25:9 indicates the 25th character position on line 9. This is a big help if you work in code because you no longer have to count character spaces to find the site of an error.

HTML 5 Output

Applies to versions 8, 9, and 10.

WebHelp was Flare's default output format for new projects for years. It's still available, but the default for new projects is now HTML5 in Flare 8-10

There's some confusion about the differences between WebHelp and HTML5 and the benefits of the latter. The About HTML5 (WebHelp 2.0) Output topic in Flare's help explains the technical advantages of HTML5. Here, I'll discuss two strategic aspects of HTML5 - supporting public-facing content and a mobile output referred to as "hybrid apps".

Public-Facing Content

If you ever put your WebHelp on a web server to make it public-facing and ran a Google search on a term in the WebHelp, you might be surprised to find that your material appears far down the search results list. That may seem odd but it also indicates a problem – users can't find your material. Instead, they're finding who-knows-what material, some of which may be wrong or even malicious. What's the problem and why does it matter?

Browser-based help has been built for years using the WebHelp format. (This format was developed by eHelp, original owner of RoboHelp.) Unlike the Microsoft-centric HTML Help, WebHelp runs on, within reason, any platform, any browser, and from any place – e.g. server, network drive, hard disk, CD, USB stick, etc. It also looks web-like. All these features brought it to its current position as the most popular output format for online help.

But WebHelp has a problem that wasn't apparent until the rise of search engines like Google. WebHelp's screen design – the horizontal toolbar frame, left-hand navigation frame, and right-hand content frame – are defined by a "frameset", a file that specifies frame elements like position, content, etc. The problem is that the frameset blocks "web crawlers" from search engines like Google that index web pages in order to generate hit lists when users do a search. The crawler can access the opening topic in your WebHelp but can't go deeper. It's like walking into a museum but being unable to go beyond the foyer. Why does this matter?

The problem is that the online help written by you, the expert, will either not appear in a search list or appear so far down the list as to go unseen. What will appear at the top is material written by people using tools that support web crawlers but that may be wrong or even malicious. In effect, using the frameset-based WebHelp means "giving up the expert space".

Whether this matters depends on your strategy regarding getting information to your users. Many companies want the information hidden behind a login and only available to people who bought the product or paid the subscription fee. But consider doing a little survey – ask your users where they look for help when they have a question. What you're concerned with is finding out how many people immediately go to Google. If many of your users do, it doesn't matter how good your frameset-based WebHelp is; it's either not available via Google or, if it is because you put it on a public-facing server, the web crawler will have trouble indexing it and the results will be so far down the search results list that users will never see it. That's where HTML5 format comes in.

Like WebHelp, HTML5 is browser-based output. The difference is that while HTML5 has a frame-like *look*, they're not controlled by a frameset – they're frameless. That lets a web crawler index all the topics in your output, making it more likely to appear in a search results list and letting you take back "the expert space".

The strategic issue here is whether you want your material to be public-facing. If you do not, and many companies don't since they want to keep control, then HTML5 has other useful benefits but openness to a web crawler isn't that important. I just suggest to such companies that they look into how many users go right to Google when they have questions, and whether not making their material public-facing and searchable (by not using HTML5 output format) may be hurting them.

Hybrid Apps

When we talk about "mobile," we're talking about three types of apps – native apps, web apps, and hybrid apps. (I'm excluding ebooks, which Flare also supports, from this discussion.)

- Native apps follow the rules of a particular platform. We refer to these apps by the name of their platform – e.g. iPhone apps, Android apps, etc. Native apps have several benefits. They're fast, and they provide programmatically simple access to "resources" on the device, like the camera and GPS. Native apps also have several drawbacks. If users have different devices, such as iPhone or Android, you have to create, test, and maintain a version for each platform. It adds expense. Each device/platform also has variants and you may have to create a version of the app for each variant – additional expense.

- Web apps can display in a browser on any device. (This also means that traditional WebHelp is effectively a web app – something to consider if you need to build tablet "apps" that display a web browser.) Web apps offset the benefits and drawbacks of native apps. You only need to create one, or a few, versions of the app since there are fewer browser variants than platform variants. However, web apps may be slower than native apps and don't provide easy access to the resources – camera, GPS, etc. – on the device. (It's harder to use the iPhone camera in a web app than in a native app.)
- Hybrid apps are a recent development that tries to use the best of native and web modes while fixing the problems.

Where Flare enters the picture is in the fact that hybrid apps are based in part on HTML5. If you output a Flare project to HTML5, the result is not a hybrid app but the code is that of a hybrid app. In other words, simply outputting to HTML5 is a step toward creating a hybrid app. I expect to see more of this hybrid app support built into later versions of Flare.

1st Heading and Title Options When Creating a New Topic

Applies to versions 8, 9, and 10.

When you create a new topic, Flare displays the Add File dialog box for a new topic, as shown below.

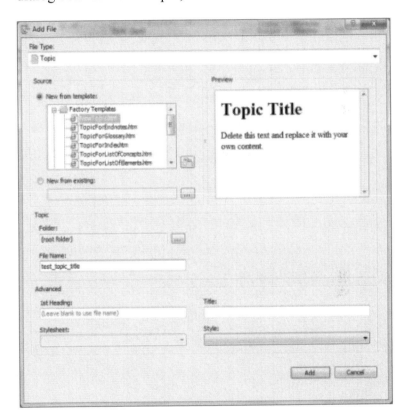

You have to type the file name in the File Name field, but the 1st Heading and Title field entries are optional. If you leave the 1st Heading field blank, Flare automatically uses the File Name entry as the 1st Heading. If you leave the Title field blank, Flare automatically uses the 1st Heading field as the title. What's the effect and why use or not use these options?

If you leave the 1st Heading field blank, Flare uses the File Name field entry as the title that users see in the topic. For example, given the file name test_topic_title and a blank 1st Heading field as shown above, the actual topic would look like this.

This is fine technically but usability is poor. It doesn't look right. Instead, you can use the same wording but make it look right by adding spaces and initial caps to the entry in the 1st Heading field, as shown below.

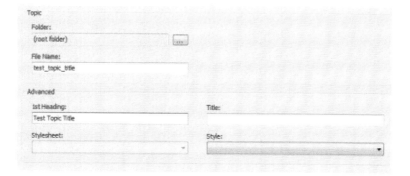

The result would look like this in the topic.

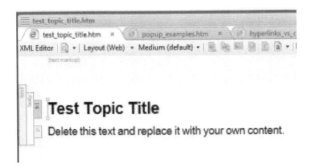

This looks like what people expect to see.

What about the Title field? If you leave the Title field blank, Flare uses the entry from the 1st Heading field for the Title field entry – e.g. the topic's 1st heading and title are identical. This seems logical; the 1st Heading, which is the title that the users see at the top of a topic, is the topic's title. But having separate 1st Heading and Title fields means that the two are technically not the same.

The 1st Heading is the text that users see at the top of a topic – it has no programmatic attributes. The Title is the 1st Heading with programmatic attributes and applies in three cases.

- Topics in the Content Explorer are listed by file name, such as test_topic_title.htm. But if you drag that topic on the TOC, the topic name apparently changes to Test Topic Title. The difference is that the Content Explorer shows the topic's file name but the TOC shows its title. If you leave the Title field blank, Flare uses the 1st Heading entry as the

Title.

This suggests that you can use a different file name and 1ˢᵗ heading for the same topic, like test_topic_title and Cocker Spaniel. You can. You can also use a different file name, 1ˢᵗ Heading, and Title for the same topic. The screen below shows an example of all three.

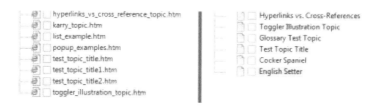

Example 1, test_topic_title, left the 1ˢᵗ Heading and Title fields blank so Flare uses the topic's file name in the TOC. This works, but you'll have to edit the TOC to turn it into real English.

Example 2, test_topic_title1, used a different but English entry for the 1ˢᵗ Heading – Cocker Spaniel. If you drag the topic from the Content Explorer to the TOC, Flare uses your 1ˢᵗ Heading entry, Cocker Spaniel, as the Title and shows that in the TOC. Notice that the 1ˢᵗ Heading, and thus the TOC entry, can be completely different from the topic's file name. The only effect will be that you'll be confused if you ever have to find this topic in Flare since you'll automatically look for a topic whose file name is, apparently, cocker_spaniel.htm, and which you won't find. You'll have to open the File List pod, find the Cocker Spaniel topic there, then find its equivalent file name. Simple but tedious.

Example 3, test_topic_title2, uses a different but English entry for the 1st Heading – Cocker Spaniel in this case, and a different value for the Title – English Setter. If you drag test_topic_title2 from the Content Explorer to the TOC, Flare uses the Title field entry English Setter in the TOC, which overrides the 1st Heading field entry and the file name and is totally confusing but technically correct.

Tip: Due to the risk of confusion from inconsistent file names, 1st Headings, and Titles for the same topic, I strongly recommend keeping them identical.

- The second case where Flare uses the Title field entry is if you open a topic in a new window or outside Flare, in Windows Explorer for example. In that case, the topic's Title field entry displays on the window title bar.
- The third case is if you add the topic to the list of topics in a "help control" link, one of the computer-controlled Related Topic link options. See the Inserting Related Topic Links topic in the Flare help for information.

Topic Templates – Creating and Adding to the Flare Interface

Applies to versions 8, 9 and 10.

A template is an item used as a model for other items of the same type. For example, you might create a topic template to use as a model when creating similar types of topics, or a master page to use when creating similar types of master pages.

Almost every feature in Flare is template based. When you create a new topic, CSS, page layout, etc., the first step is to select the template on which to base the new item. Below, for example, is the dialog box that displays when you add a topic. Note the "Source" options in the upper left corner.

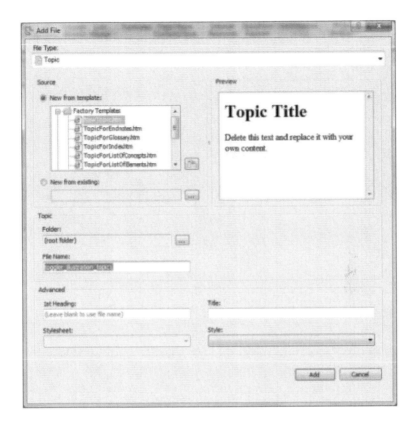

Flare automatically uses a default factory template for any item you create. In the image above, for example, that template for a new topic is NewTopic.htm in the Factory Templates group. The Preview window at the right side of the dialog box shows what the default NewTopic.htm template looks like. But what if you want to use your own custom template instead of Flare's default? For example, say you want to create and use your own template for creating task description topics.

If you scrolled down the template list shown in the image above, you'd come to this...

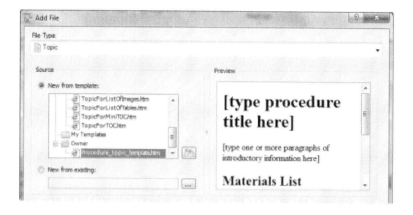

Here, the Owner folder contains one template called Procedure_ topic_template.htm. Selecting that template gives the preview shown on the right of the image.

You *could* simply create a topic called Procedure Topic Template and add it to your project. Then, for any new topic that you want to create and base on the template topic, you'd copy the template topic, rename the copy, and edit the copy to create the real topic. This is simple but has one huge flaw – eventually you'll forget to make a copy of the template and will overwrite it.

A better way is to create a template and make it part of the Flare interface. That way, it will always be available and can't be overwritten.

The following description explains how to create topic templates but actually applies to any new element in Flare – topics, page layouts, master pages, CSSs, etc. It's a three-step process.

1. Create and structure the topic using prompts and fixed heads to make the template-to-be as self-documenting as possible. (You can put prompts in square brackets – e.g. [This is a prompt...] to make them easy to spot and tell the author exactly what to enter.)

   Tip: Give the template-to-be a name that clearly defines its purpose, like "task topic template."

2. Select, or create, the folder to hold the templates. This will be a top-level folder. When you create a new template and save it, Flare will create the appropriately-named subfolder in the templates folder.

Tip: This is easy but it's easy to make one common mistake – forgetting to specify the top-level folder when you create the template-to-be and then having to go find it. It's more of a slap-your-forehead mistake than anything serious. Just pay attention to where you saved the template.

3. Add the template-to-be to Flare's interface by accessing the Template Manager. To do this, either:

   - Select the Tools menu item and the Manage Templates option in the Templates group near the center of the ribbon, or
   - Click the Manage Templates icon in the Source area on the dialog box for the element you're creating. For example, for the New Topic dialog box:

In either case, the Template Manager dialog box opens.

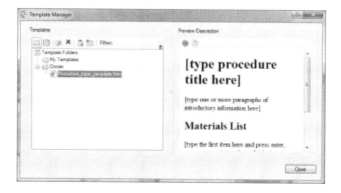

Assuming you already created the folder to contain the template and the template-to-be itself, click on the folder name, click the Add Template File 📑 icon, select the template-to-be from the Open dialog box, and click Open. The Save As Template dialog box opens, shown below.

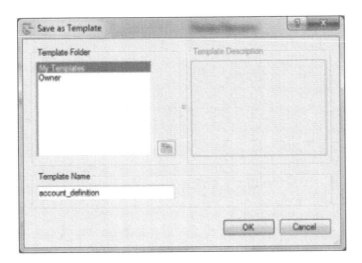

Select the folder to contain the template in the Template
Folder list. Change the template name in the Template
Name field if necessary.

Tip: If you create a template-to-be and name it
descriptively from the start, such as "task_topic_template",
you shouldn't have to rename it. You're more likely to
have to rename a template if you decided to use a real topic
as a template and need to change its name from the topic
name to a more general template name.

Toggler Links

Applies to versions 8, 9, and 10.

A toggler is a specialized type of dropdown. In a dropdown, the body text can only display in one chunk immediately below the hotspot. However, in a toggler, the body text can display in separate chunks anywhere in a topic. Here are some examples to make this clearer, starting with the raw topic, below.

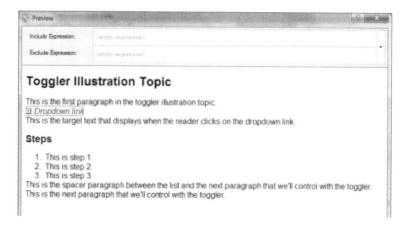

Notice the raw material for a dropdown link, the second and third paragraphs. The next image shows those paragraphs converted to a dropdown link, first collapsed.

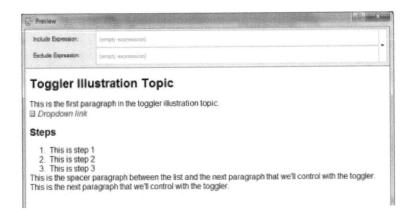

Then expanded, shown below.

Again, the dropdown body can only appear below the hotspot. The toggler eliminates this restriction. Body chunks can be anywhere. For example, note the Advanced Material link at the top of the topic in the next image, and the fact that the steps and last paragraph have disappeared. Note also that the arrow in the icon to the left of the toggler link is pointing to the right.

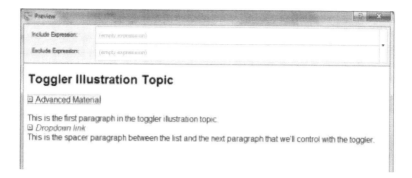

Clicking on the Advanced Material link displays the body, the list of steps and the paragraph, in two chunks, as shown below, and the icon arrow is now pointing down.

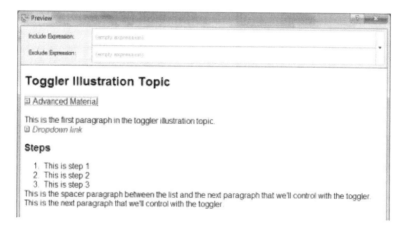

To recap, a toggler can hide or show material anywhere, not just immediately below the hotspot.

Why use togglers? Two possibilities:

- Show or hide different kinds of information in topics. Say that the description of a process contains both basic and advanced material but you don't want to show both at the same time for fear of confusing new users.

You could put the advanced material in its own topic and link to it from the basic topic. That works, but makes it difficult to write the advanced material because you're writing it out of context.

You could also create a separate dropdown for each piece of advanced material. This keeps the advanced material in context but may require creating many drop-downs.

A toggler eliminates both problems by letting you create one "switch," the toggler, which hides or shows all that advanced material with one click.

- Show or hide different categories of information in a topic, similar to the previous example but with a twist. Say that the light and full versions of your product offer different features and you want to be able to modify the list of features depending on whether the reader selects light or full. You could create one bulleted list of features but create a toggler that hides the full-version's features if the reader clicks a "light" link and shows the full-version's features if the reader clicks the "full" link.

How do you create a toggler? It's a three-step process.

1. Create the topic with all the content – that which you want displayed by default when the topic opens and that which you want to display only when users click the toggler link.

    This is standard topic creation, although you'll want to consider which content elements will be "togglerized" when you plan the topic.

2. Assign a name to each content element (image, steps, paragraph, etc.) whose display will be controlled by the toggler – e.g. will be hidden until users click the toggler link.
To assign a name to an element, click on the element in the topic, and then either:

- Select the Home menu item and select the Name option in the Attributes group toward the right hand side of the ribbon, or
- Right-click the block bar for the element and select Name.

In each case, the Manage Named Elements dialog box opens.

The dialog box lets you add a new name and shows the currently assigned names, each named element's style tag, and its content.

Now type the name for the new element.

Tip: You can use the same name for multiple elements in a topic but it's easier to keep track of named elements in a topic if you give them different names. For example, instead of using "steps" as the name for two separate lists, you might name the two lists "steps – wash" and "steps – rinse".

3. Create the toggler link by typing the toggler link text and specifying which named information elements to display when the reader clicks the link. To assign the named elements to the toggler link, highlight the toggler link text, select the Insert menu item, and select the Toggler option in the Text group toward the right hand side of the ribbon. The Insert Toggler dialog box opens.

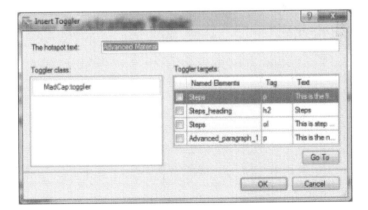

Click in the checkboxes for the named elements to be controlled by the toggler, then click OK. Those elements will no longer be visible in preview mode or output until the user clicks the toggler.

Master Pages vs. Page Layouts

Applies to versions 8, 9, and 10.

The difference between a master page and a page layout can be confusing. The PDF target editor's General tab, shown below, is also confusing since it asks you to specify the Master Page Layout. Is it referring to a master page, a page layout, or a combination of the two?

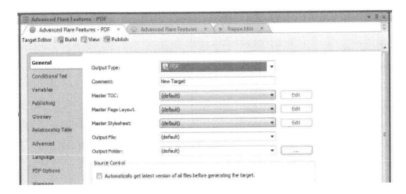

Master Pages

A master page is a "super-template" for online outputs but not for print outputs. Anything on a master page appears on every topic in the output. For example, the image below shows a topic in a project with no master page.

Note that there's no header or footer in the topic. The next image shows the same topic but with a master page that adds a header "My Company" and the breadcrumb trail – the "You are here" – at the top of the topic.

The header and breadcrumb trail were added in a master page that was then applied to the target. (To select the master page for a target, use the Master Page field on the Advanced tab in the target editor for that particular target.)

This feature is potentially very useful since it lets you define and assign a header and/or footer to every topic in an output by just defining those elements once, in the master page. (The master page can also contain a breadcrumb trail and other elements.)

What can you put in a header or footer? Almost anything. Text is common, like a company name and address or a copyright, but you might also put a table containing the topic content's sign-off history, links, images, and more. For a good example, open any topic in the Flare help and look at the top and bottom of the topic, like the one shown below.

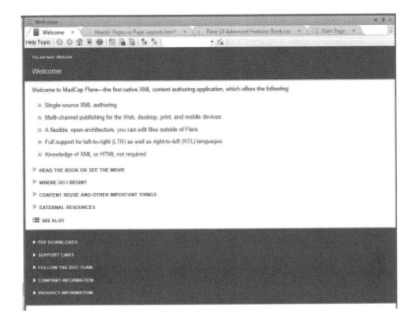

The header at the top contains the breadcrumb trail, the "You are here..." The footer is more involved, with links to company, product, and support information, social media "follow-me" links, and links to downloadable PDF files.

It's a lot of work to add this to one topic. To add it to multiple topics is worse. But by adding all this information to a master page, the information gets applied to each topic in the output.

Two notes about using master pages:

- In theory, you can only use one master page per output target. (The Master Page field on the Advanced tab of the Target Editor only lets you select one master page.) However, there may be times when you want to use two or more master pages in one output target. For example, you might be generating a target containing material that refers to different modules of a product and want to use different headers for each module. You can do so, and get around the Master Page field limit, by using a feature of the Stylesheet editor. To do so, open the knowledge base at kb.madcapsoftware.com and see the two topics under Flare/Masterpages on the TOC.

- You can create templates for almost any feature in Flare, such as topic templates. For example, you might define concept, task, and reference topic templates as a way to get consistency among multiple topics of each type. If you do this and apply a master page too, don't put the same information in the topic templates and the master page or else that information will be duplicated in each topic, once from the master page and once from the template. It's a minor mistake and easy to fix, but it's also an easy mistake to not make.

Page Layouts

Page layouts apply to print outputs like Word and PDF. An easy way to understand them is to compare them to Word's Page Setup feature – they let you define print properties like page size, orientation, and margins. You can define different properties for the title page, odd and even pages, and more.

Page layouts are confusing because they offer so many options. (MadCap increased the number of features a few releases ago, apparently to compete with Framemaker, and has continued to add features with each new release of Flare.) For example, the image below shows a simple page layout with only the header specified.

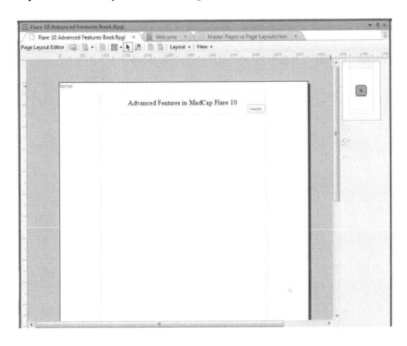

The next screen shows the Page Properties dialog box open for the same page layout.

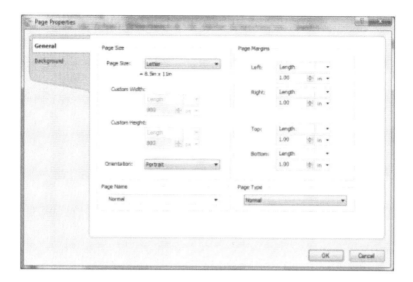

The next screen shows the Frame Properties dialog box for the same page layout.

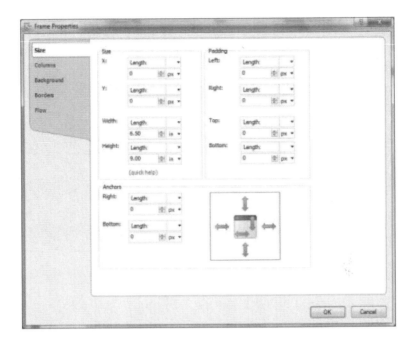

There are many print features besides page layouts. If you need more than simple print output, see the downloadable PDF Print-Based output Guide.

Linked vs Unlinked Table of Contents Headings

Applies to versions 8, 9 and 10.

You can set up the headings in a table of contents in two ways, linked or unlinked.

- Clicking an unlinked heading expands it to show all the topics and subheadings under that heading. Users can then click on any topic under that heading to display it. Clicking on the expanded heading closes it.
  For example, the image below shows a table of contents with the unlinked heading "Spreadsheet Concepts" that's collapsed.

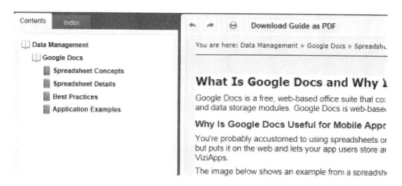

The image below shows the same table of contents with that heading expanded.

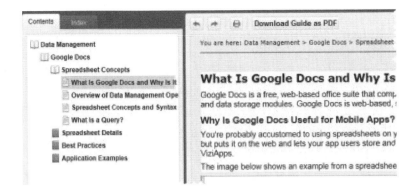

Clicking on the heading expanded it but didn't change the topic displayed in the right pane.

- Clicking a linked heading expands it *and* opens a topic to which the heading is linked. This might be a topic that introduces the content under the heading. Users can then click on any topic under the heading in order to display it. Clicking the expanded linked heading closes it and again displays the topic to which the heading is linked.

For example, the image below shows the table of contents with the linked heading "Spreadsheet Concepts" collapsed. The help system is showing the last topic that was opened.

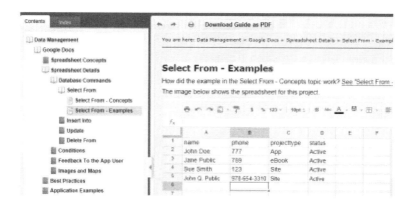

The image below shows the same table of contents with the linked heading expanded and a new topic displayed, the one to which the "Spreadsheet Concepts" heading is linked.

Users can now navigate to whatever topic they want by clicking it in the table of contents.

Clicking on the heading again collapses that section of the table of contents and displays the same topic, in this case "Introduction to Spreadsheet Concepts", again.

To recap - the unlinked method means that clicking on a table of contents heading expands or collapses that heading. The linked method means that clicking on a table of contents heading expands or collapses that heading *and* displays a topic linked to that heading.

A few points about these options:

- Some authors like the linked method because they can add an introductory topic for a section of the table of contents and have that topic open every time users click on the heading for that section. Other authors don't like the method because users have to click on that heading again to close that section of the table of contents. When they do, the same topic opens again.

  Because of that, many authors use the unlinked method and just add an introductory topic as the first topic under that heading. That way, users only see the introductory topic once, if they want to. Otherwise, they can ignore it.

- The TOC Editor has a feature that can help authors who want to use the linked heading method. That's the Show Unlinked Books icon, shown below.

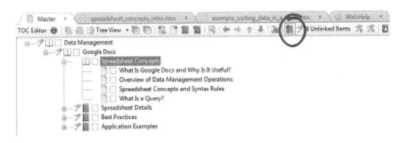

The unlinked items field, next to the Show Unlinked Books icon, shows all unlinked entries in the table of contents. The Show Unlinked Books icon specifically shows all unlinked headings. If you want to link headings to topics, then you'll want to know which ones are not yet linked. Selecting this icon adds a yellow flag to the left of each unlinked heading. If you don't want to link headings to topics, then you don't need the information from the Show Unlinked Books icon and can deselect that option.

Relative vs Absolute Units of Measure for Styles

Applies to versions 8, 9, and 10.

When you define a style's size, you'll see options like Ems, X-Height, and Percentage that may be unfamiliar. What are they and why use them? First, some background.

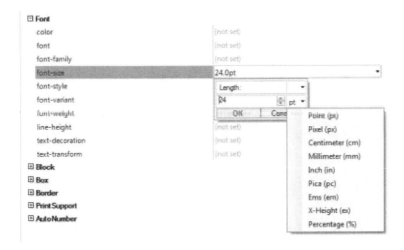

Point (pt) is the best known and most easily understand option. It comes from the print world where 72pt equals one inch, so 12pt text = 1/6", and is a fixed, or absolute, unit. It's fine for fixed page sizes but problematic in browser-based output like WebHelp or HTML5 that may have to run in different browsers on different devices with different display technologies. The problem is that text in points can't be resized by a browser and can't be resized by a browser user (by selecting View > Text Size in IE).

To illustrate the issue, look at Windows vs. the Mac.

PCs and Macs use different display technologies that make 10pt text legible on a PC but hard to read on a Mac, where 12pt might be more appropriate. Now imagine that you're creating browser-based output that might be read on a PC or a Mac. What size do you use for normal text, 10pt or 12pt? You can use two CSSs but that's inefficient. Instead, use one style sheet but set the text size using a relative unit – Percentage, Ems, or X-Height.

- Percentage (%) – Based on the default size for normal in each browser's font set, 100%. Other sizes are relative to that. For example, an h1 of 150% makes it half again as large as normal on each browser. The drawback is that you can't say what size that really is if you think in print terms, but the benefit is that you've offloaded the work of sizing control to the individual browsers.

- Ems (em) – Based on the height of the uppercase M for each browser's font set. 1 em = 100%, 1.5 em = 150%, half again as large as normal. The drawback and benefit are the same as for the Percentage (%) option, so the choice of Percentage vs. Ems is a matter of preference.
- X-Height (ex) – Based on the height of the lowercase x for each browser's font set. The drawback and benefit are the same as for the other two options but this option is not well supported by browsers. Don't use it unless you have some unusual need.

So should you use relative units of measure for style sizes?

- If all you're creating is print, you can stick with points.
- If you're creating browser-based output for one platform, you can still use points. You just won't get the cross-platform/cross-browser flexibility (but you may not care) and users won't be able to resize your text in IE.
- If you're creating cross-platform/cross-browser output, and/or want to start future-proofing your output, then start using relative units.

The choice is up to you. I prefer Percentage (%) because I find it easier to understand a size like 150% than 1.5 ems, but that's simply my preference.

Unbind

Applies to versions 8, 9, and 10.

When working with features like dropdown links, expanding text links, topic popups, and lists, you'll see an "Unbind" option in some of the dialog boxes option lists. For example, if you create a dropdown link and right-click on its block bar, you'll see the list of options shown below.

Clicking "unbind" removes the dropdown or other effect from the text but keeps the text itself - e.g. converts the text back to plain text. It's less trouble than having to physically delete the text with the effect and then retype the text itself.

Hyperlinks vs. Cross-References

Applies to versions 8, 9, and 10.

Hyperlinks are the standard navigation tool for help systems and have been with us for over two decades. But hyperlinks have a problem – they're "stupid". They point to a target position but have no awareness of what's at that position. For example, let's say that topic A contains a hyperlink that points to topic B that describes milkshakes. The result looks like this, in topic A...

Clicking the link takes the reader here, to topic B...

But what happens if you change the name of the Milkshake topic to Frappe? The link still works but it looks like this...

The link seems to be going to the wrong topic – one dealing with something called a frappe. It's the right topic – frappe is simply a regional term for milkshake – but it looks confusing.

Now assume that we create the link but use a cross-reference in place of the hyperlink. You don't have to select the text to link. In fact, you don't *want to* select the text because the cross-reference text will overwrite the selected original text. Instead, simply add a place for a "see" reference, like the one in the parentheses at the end of the second sentence in the image below.

Clicking the See "Milkshake" cross-reference opens the topic like the hyperlink did. However, let's say you now change the name of the Milkshake topic to Frappe. When you generate the output or select the Update Cross-

References option on the Tools menu ribbon, the see...
reference changes to this...

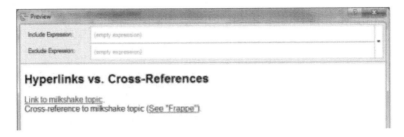

In other words, the text of the cross-reference changed to
match the changed title of the target topic. (Note that the
text still refers to the milkshake topic. You'd either have to
change the word "milkshake" to "frappe" by hand or
replace it with a variable.)

The example above used the target topic's title, but you can
also link cross-references to bookmarks within the body of
a topic. (If you've used cross-references in MS Word,
Flare's "cross-reference linked to a bookmark" feature will
look familiar.) For example, the topic below has a
bookmark at the start of the second paragraph – the
rhode_island bookmark. (It's displayed because the Show
Markers option under the Show Tags icon on the XML
Editor toolbar is selected.)

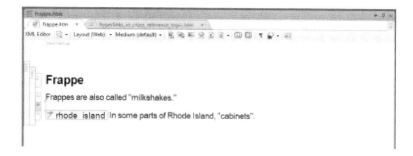

Note the effect on the cross-reference link text in the image below.

The cross-reference is using the text flagged by the bookmark. You can control this by controlling the format of the bookmark code itself.

Why use cross-references instead of hyperlinks?

- Cross-reference wording is "aware of" the target text and changes if you change that text, simplifying maintenance.
- Cross-reference formatting is controlled by the Flare <MadCap | xref> style. That makes it easy to establish a consistent wording for all "links" by formatting them using that style, such as specifying that all cross-references use the format "See <text>"

and then, if you decide that you don't like that format, change it globally by changing the properties of the <MadCap | xref> style in the CSS.

- Cross-reference styles can differ in different outputs. For example, you can specify that your cross-reference links use the format "See <text>" for online outputs but "See <text> on page <pagenumber>" for printed outputs. (See the next section in this book.)

Why not use cross-references instead of hyperlinks?

- Cross-references are conceptually more complex than traditional hyperlinks. New Flare developers can easily understand hyperlinks but cross-references require a mental adjustment. However, the adjustment should be quick.
- Cross-references are not W3C-compliant. This may be important if your company follows W3C standards.

Whether or not you decide to use cross-references, they're worth investigating and trying – especially if you plan to generate print outputs to paper.

Format Cross-References to Show Page Numbers in Printed Output

Applies to versions 8, 9, and 10.

Cross-references are useful but have one problem when used in a print format that's physically printed - the links don't work. Consider the example below.

If you output this to an online format, the link works. Output to a print format like PDF and view it online and the link works. But when you print the output, the link obviously can't work. So how do users follow the reference?

You *could* make sure that the link always refers to a target by the title of its topic and have a table of contents as part of the output. That way, users see the reference to "Frappe", turn to the table of contents, find "Frappe", (which may be hard to do in a long table of contents), find the page number, and turn to that page. This approach works but is cumbersome for the users.

There is another approach that can convert the reference from a link style to a page-reference like 'See "Frappe" on page 73'. It's surprisingly easy. Just select the Print medium for the MadCap | xref style in the CSS. This tells Flare to use the 'See "Frappe"' format for online output but change it to 'See "Frappe" on page 73' format for print output.

For example, here's the format of the MadCap | xref style in the CSS for the Default medium.

And here it is with the medium changed to Print.

Changing the medium to "Print" adds "on page {page}" code that tells Flare to add the words "on page" and calculate and show the page number where the target appears. The result in the output looks like this for online:

Configuring Active Edit

The active edit feature allows you to edit remote files quickly and without having to

To configure an extension for active edit (See "What Is WS FTP"):

1. In the toolbar, click **Options**, then select the **Active Edit** dialog.

And like this for print:

Configuring Active Edit

The active edit feature allows you to edit remote files quickly and without having to actively transfer them first.

To configure an extension for active edit (See "What Is WS_FTP" on page 2):

1. In the toolbar, click **Options**, then select the **Active Edit** dialog.

You can modify the cross-reference format by using the Cross-Reference Format dialog box, shown below. To access it, click on the entry field for mc-format for the MadCap | xref style.

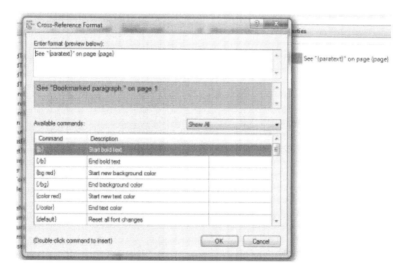

This dialog box offers almost unlimited format control but, again, at a minimum, all you have to do is change the medium from Default to Print to get a perfectly fine cross-reference format for print output.

Manually Update Cross-References

Applies to versions 8, 9, and 10.

If you change a cross-reference's target name, Flare updates the cross-reference when you generate the output. Until then, it can be confusing to see the old target name in the cross-reference when you know that you changed the name. You can fix this at any time by forcing the updating of the cross-references. To do so, select the Tools menu item and the Update Cross-References option toward the right hand side of the ribbon.

How to Create and Use Mediums

Applies to versions 8, 9, and 10.

Suppose you're creating a project to be output as WebHelp and decide that h1 should be Verdana, 16 pt, blue. Easy. Specify those settings for the h1 style in the CSS.

Now suppose you need to output that same project to PDF and decide that h1 should be Verdana, 16 pt, black. Easy. Specify those settings for the h1 style in the CSS.

But you already specified h1 as blue for the WebHelp output, so you have to modify the h1 color setting in the CSS depending on whether you're outputting WebHelp or PDF. This works, but you'll forget to make the change eventually and will generate WebHelp with the PDF settings and vice versa.

The answer *seems to be* to use two CSSs, one called online and one called PDF for example, that are identical except for the h1 settings. This works but is inefficient since you're maintaining two CSSs for the sake of one style setting. And things will get worse if you add additional outputs with their own individual settings, such as mobile, where you might want h1 to be Verdana, 11 pt, bold, blue, for example. You need a third CSS, and still another one each time you add an output. Mediums offer a better way.

A medium is an alternate set of properties for a particular style. For example, using the h1 example above, let's say you need to define h1 styles for three different output targets. Instead of creating three CSSs, you create one and pick a default output, such as WebHelp. You then specify that h1 for the default output is Verdana, 16 pt, blue. But you then specify an alternate set of properties for print output; "print" is a medium and the print medium's settings for h1 are Verdana, 16 pt, black, bold. You also specify an alternate set of properties for mobile output; "mobile" is a medium and the mobile medium settings for h1 are Verdana, 11 pt, bold, blue. None of the other styles' settings change.

How does this work in theory?

If you're generating the default WebHelp output, tell Flare to use the default CSS settings. But if you're generating print output, tell Flare to use the default CSS settings but use the print medium wherever it's been applied. It's only been applied to one style, h1, so h1 uses the properties defined for the print medium rather than for the default medium. The same holds true for the mobile medium. So you can have as many output targets as you want, all under the control of one CSS with just a few changes defined by the mediums.

How does this work, in practice?

Mediums are controlled, except for deletion, in the Stylesheet Editor. When you open the Stylesheet Editor, you'll see the Mediums field and dropdown on the toolbar, as shown, with the dropdown open, in the image below.

Flare comes with three pre-defined mediums – default, non-print, and print. The "default-vs-non-print" options can get confusing. Some authors decide that WebHelp is their default output and just use the default medium. Other authors decide that WebHelp is their default output but use the non-print medium. Both choices work. Just be sure that the next author can understand what you did.

For illustration, I'll go with the default medium approach. You want to set h1's properties for the default output to Comic Sans, 16 pt, red, so set the medium selection to default, scroll down to h1 in the Styles list on the left, expand the Font Properties group, and make the desired settings, as shown below.

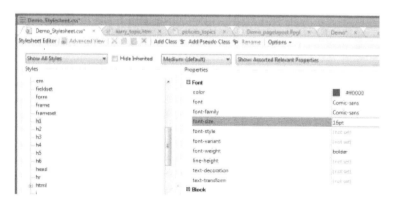

Now to set the h1's properties for PDF. (You can add a medium called PDF or just use the print medium.) The image below shows the medium set to print, h1 selected in the Styles list on the left, and the Font Properties group expanded, with the desired settings for print.

This defines both sets of properties for h1 in one CSS. The last step is to save.

How do you see the result during development and how do you apply them to the finished output?

To see the result during development, open a topic to which that CSS has been applied and note which medium it's using, shown in the Medium field on the XML Editor's toolbar. In the image below, the default medium is in effect and h1, the topic title, is in 16pt, red.

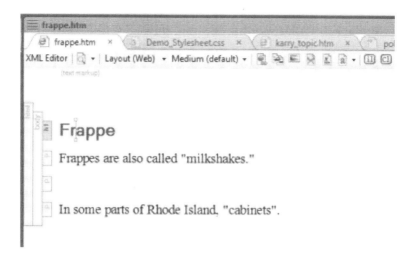

In the image below, the medium is now print and the topic title is now in whatever color you selected for print, black in my example.

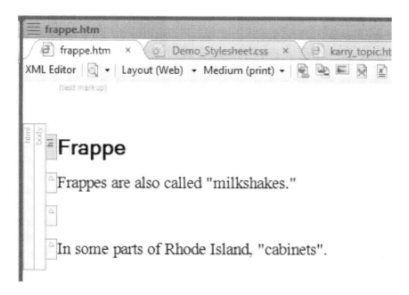

The change affects every topic to which the CSS was applied. A medium is like a switch. Turn it to one position and one set of style properties gets used. Turn it to a different position and a different set of properties gets used. It's a very useful feature because it lets you tailor all the topics in a project for a particular output at one time.

How do you apply a medium to a given output? Open the Target Editor for that target, go to the Advanced tab, and select the medium in the Medium field.

Several notes about working with mediums:

- First, a caution. It's easy to change the medium setting from default to the one that you want to modify, modify the properties for that medium, and go on with your work without switching the medium back to default. At some point, you're going to want to make some changes to the styles, open the Stylesheet Editor, make your changes, and not understand why the changes aren't working. It's invariably because you forgot to change the medium setting in the Stylesheet Editor back to default and you're making your changes in the wrong medium.

Tip: Whenever working with mediums, define any extra mediums that you need, define all their settings, and then set the medium field in the Stylesheet Editor back to default.

- To create a new medium, open the Stylesheet Editor, select the pulldown for the Options field on the right side of the Stylesheet Editor toolbar, select Add Medium, and name the new medium. It will immediately appear in the Medium field dropdown.

How to Delete Mediums

Applies to versions 8, 9 and 10.

Mediums are easy to work with via the Flare interface except for one thing, deletion. Let's say you added a medium for an output target that you no longer support or you were just experimenting. In each case, there are unused mediums cluttering the interface. The image below, for example, shows a custom medium called Neil that you're no longer using.

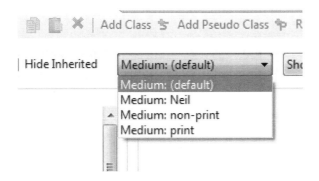

Deleting a medium is one of the few cases in which you must go into the code for the CSS file. You can't delete a medium via the interface, although it's a feature request. To delete the medium:

1. Open the Stylesheets folder under the Resources folder on the Content Explorer.
2. Right-click on the stylesheet containing the medium to delete and select Open With > Internal Text Editor.

3. Search for the characters @media and the name of the medium, such as @media Neil
4. Select and delete everything from @media name to and including the closing right curly brace (}).

In the image below, for example, the Neil media type has no properties set for it so you'd just delete from the media type to the closing curly brace. The type above the Neil media type, print, has some properties set for the h1 style so you'd have to delete from @media print to the closing curly brace *after* the h1 setting.

```
25 }
26
27 @media print
28 {
29     h1
30     {
31         color: #000000;
32     }
33 }
34
35 @media Neil
36 {
37
38 }
39
```

5. Save and close the code view of the CSS file.

When you click the Medium dropdown in the Stylesheet Editor, the selected medium will be gone.

Change the Display of Style Properties on the Stylesheet Editor

Applies to versions 8, 9, and 10.

Flare's Stylesheet Editor is very powerful, especially in Advanced mode (even with no property group expanded), as shown below.

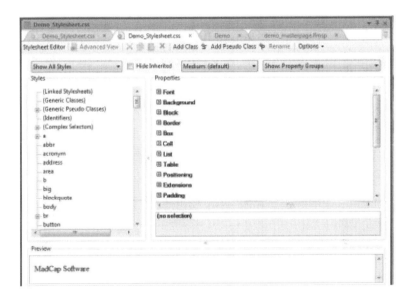

Expanding any property group can increase the confusion. For example, here's the Stylesheet Editor with h1 selected and the Font property group expanded.

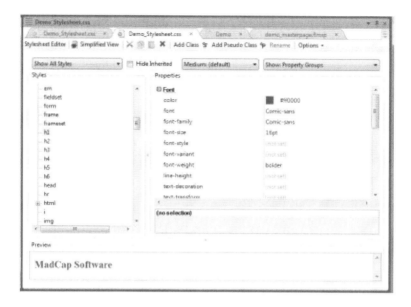

You can gauge the number of options available by looking at the size of the elevator box and realizing that there are nineteen other property groups that are not expanded. It's a lot of options.

To add to the confusion, some properties are duplicated in different property groups. For example, both the Box and Cell groups offer padding options but it's not clear if they're the same padding options used in two places or different padding options. To further confuse things, there's also a separate Padding property group.

To help you, Flare offers five ways to list the property options via the Show option on the Stylesheet Editor toolbar, shown below.

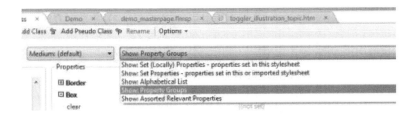

- Set (Locally) Properties… - Lists only the style properties that have been specifically set in one or more topics and that thus override the default settings for those styles. It also hides styles whose properties have not been set.

- Set Properties… - Lists all the style properties set for the styles.
- Alphabetical List – Alphabetically lists all the properties, which means that each property appears only once in the list no matter how many times it's used in different groups of properties. For example, the padding options only appear once because there's only one of each even though they appear in three property groups.
- Property Groups – Lists all properties by functional group. This means that some properties, like padding, appear several times because they apply to multiple functions.
- Assorted Relevant Properties – Lists the property groups that MadCap considers most relevant for a style. This may hide a property you're looking for but it reduces the number of options, simplifying an often intimidating task.

For example, the image below shows the listing by Property Groups.

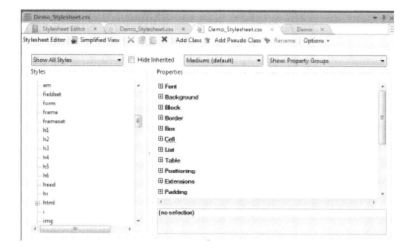

The image below shows the listing by Assorted Relevant Properties.

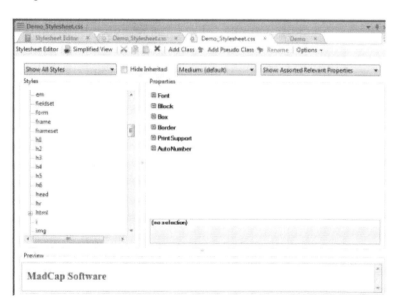

The latter is obviously simpler to use and should meet all but the most complex style setting needs.

How Flare's Styles Pane Differs From Other HATs and Word

Applies to versions 8, 9, and 10.

New Flare authors sometimes complain that the Styles pane, on the right side of the screen in the image below, doesn't behave consistently. It seems to list different styles at different times for no apparent reason.

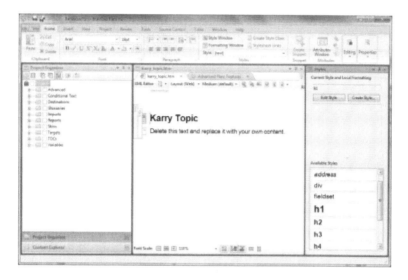

In the image above, for example, the Styles pane lists styles like div, fieldset, h1, h2, etc., but in the image below it lists styles like abbr, acronym, b, etc.

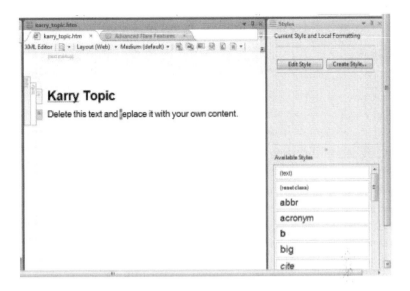

What's going on?

Flare is really trying to help. Until recently, most authoring tools showed *all* available styles when you opened the list of styles. This meant that you had to sort through a long, cumbersome list of styles to find the one you wanted.

Flare tries to eliminate this problem by listing only the styles that apply to your location in the file. For example, if you do not select any text, as shown in the first image in this section, or select an entire paragraph's worth of text, Flare lists paragraph styles. But if you select anything less than a whole paragraph, such as selecting one word or even a single character, as shown in the image above, Flare lists character styles. This shortens the list of styles from which to choose at any given time and, once you get used to it, simplifies your work.

Local Formatting and the Styles Pane

Applies to versions 8, 9, and 10.

When I discuss styles and stylesheets, people typically understand the use of styles for headings but assume they'll still do local formatting, like bold and italics, by using the formatting options on the Home menu item ribbon – "local" or "inline" formatting. This assumption arises because we've used the local formatting options for so long that it's hard to break the habit.

As noted in the section on See "How Flare's Styles Pane Differs From Other HATs and Word", we can do local formatting using the Styles pane by selecting a word or a sentence – anything less than a full paragraph – and formatting it using the character styles on the Styles pane, as shown in the image below.

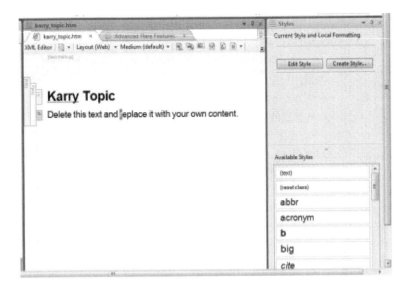

So boldfacing a word by selecting it and clicking the b option on the Styles pane gives the same result as clicking the B icon in the Font group on the Home menu item ribbon.

If you scroll down the character styles on the Styles pane, you'll see various other styles, some familiar like I and some odd like code and tt. The odder ones date to the early days of HTML and are rarely used, but they are still available.

Why is the issue of local formatting important? Two reasons - design philosophy and code-level flexibility:

- Design – In the early days of the web, all formatting was local. Developers would specify settings for things like fonts, font weight, etc. in the HTML files. (Flare uses XHTML, not HTML. XHTML is basically HTML but uses the syntax rules of XML – hence XHTML – and is very similar.) However, the trend over the last decade has been to move all formatting out of the HTML (topic) files and into a separate CSS file. The less format code in the topic files, the easier the files are to work with, the easier it is to make large-scale changes to a help system, and the easier it is to convert between formats. So there's a strategic rationale for doing formatting through the CSS.

- Code – At first glance, boldfacing words by clicking the B icon in the Font group on the Home menu ribbon versus using the b option on the Styles pane, for example, has the same effect. But consider this (real) scenario.

A bank is writing online help for an investment analysis package and wants to indicate the degree of risk of an investment by formatting it as bold green (safe), bold yellow (risky), or bold red (avoid). You could do that by highlighting each investment and formatting it locally as bold and green, yellow, or red. Fifty times each… But what happens if the client decides that the shade of yellow you used doesn't stand out and wants it darker? You'd have to highlight and re-color fifty instances. Now, let's say that instead of local formatting, you create three character styles called Safe, Risky, and Avoid, and made each one bold and the appropriate color. By assigning the Risky style to those investments and then changing the shade of yellow for the Risky style, you change all fifty at once. This is far more efficient.

There is one oddity to replacing local formatting with styles. You might assume that assigning styles from the stylesheet will insert different code than you'd get by using the B icon on the ribbon. In fact, each way gives the same code – formatted word for boldfacing, for example. So what's the point?

You're seeing one of the bumps in the evolution of standards. A few years ago, Flare actually inserted different codes depending on whether you were doing true local formatting or applying the b style. However, there was a problem with the W3C (WorldWide Web Consortium) code that got inserted as a style and MadCap reverted to inserting the same code each way until the issue gets settled. So for the moment, it doesn't matter technically. But it's still a good idea to start replacing local formatting with character styles from the stylesheet so that you'll get into the habit of doing it right once the code standards settle down.

List Styles - Applying

Applies to versions 8, 9 and 10.

Since Flare's Styles pane only displays the styles that apply to your position in a topic, how do you make Flare display list styles? In the image below, for example, the topic contains entries that you want to turn into bulleted and numbered lists. But when you look at the styles on the Styles pane, there are no list styles available.

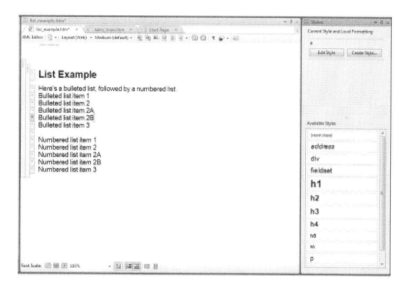

If the stylesheet doesn't show list styles, how do you create a list? Remember that Flare displays styles relevant to your position in a topic. Right now, the two "lists" are just text in quasi-list form but not "real" lists. So the first step is to make them real lists by selecting the appropriate list option in the Paragraph group on the Home menu ribbon.

In the example below, I've applied the bullet list option to the first five items in the list-to-be.

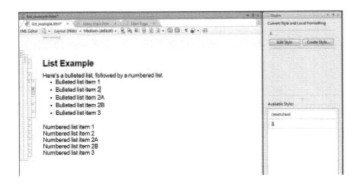

Notice the change in the Styles pane. Flare now "knows" that this list really is a list, specifically a bulleted list. (Selecting the bullet list option added <ul></ul> tags to the entire list and an <li></li> tag to each bullet item. ul is the code for an unordered list – e.g. a bulleted list and li is the code for a list item.) The Styles pane can now display all the list style tags in the stylesheet for this project, in this case only the basic, default list item style – li.

The image below is a more realistic example from a real project.

The Styles pane now lists the same default li style but adds three bulleted list styles, two numbered list styles, and a TBLhead style (that doesn't apply to this discussion). Ideally, you would have created these styles in the stylesheet before the project began.

You may have another problem with bulleted and numbered lists. How do you create an unbulleted or unnumbered continuation paragraph after a bulleted or numbered item? For example, how to add an unnumbered explanatory paragraph after a numbered step? You can add the paragraph, then turn off its numbering and adjust the indent to match that of the numbered step, but this is very inefficient. There are two better ways.

- The "proper" way is to add a style called something like "Level 1 continuation" to the stylesheet and define this style's properties as having no number and an indent equal to the indent of the level 1 numbered style.
  Using this approach, you type the numbered item, press Enter, type the unnumbered item-to-be, which gets the next number, click in the unnumbered item-to-be, and select the continuation style. This keeps the indent but turns off the numbering.
- The "improper" but often-used way is to place the pointer at the end of the numbered item, press Shift/Enter to add a "soft return" that keeps the numbered item's indent but doesn't number it, press Shift/Enter again and type the unnumbered paragraph, press Shift/Enter again to add a blank line, and finally press Enter to add a "hard return" and turn the numbering back on. In the long run, this is not a good approach but many people use it because it's so simple.

Numbered List "Continuation" Style

Applies to versions 8, 9, and 10.

If you create topics containing numbered lists, you may need to add unnumbered "continuation paragraphs" after items in a numbered list, like the one after item 2 below:

1. This is the first item in the numbered list.
2. This is the second item in the list.
   This paragraph discusses the second list item. It has to have the same indent as the numbered item to which it refers, should not be numbered, and should not mess up the number sequence for the item that follows.
3. This is the third item in the list.

How do you get this effect?

People often just add the continuation paragraph to-be as a numbered item, turn off its numbering, reset the indent, and fix the number of the next numbered item. This works, but it's slow and inefficient.

A somewhat better idea is to add the continuation paragraph using "soft returns," created by pressing Shift/Enter after the numbered item. You'd press Shift/Enter to add a blank line after the numbered item, Shift/Enter again to add the line for the paragraph, type the paragraph, press Shift/Enter to end the paragraph, and a final Shift/Enter to add a blank line after the paragraph.

Pressing Enter then adds the next, correctly numbered, item.

The soft return approach works but it's local formatting. The much better alternative is to create and use a "continuation" style instead. That provides the efficiency of styles in general and is a best-practice.

Creating a continuation style is mechanically simple but can be confusing if you're not familiar with the Stylesheet editor. Here's how to do it.

1. Open your CSS in the Stylesheet editor in Advanced view.
2. Select Show All Styles in the list box in the upper left corner of the Stylesheet editor.
3. Right-click on the li style and select Add Class. The New Style dialog box opens.
4. Call the new style numlist_continue_1 or something like that. Any name will do as long as it's clear that the style is for creating a continuation paragraph and is to be used for level 1 numbered lists. (This also tells you that you can create continuation styles for lower level numbered lists by simply changing their left indents.)
5. Select Show: Property Groups in the list box in the upper right corner of the Stylesheet editor.
6. Open the List property group for your new style and set list_style_type to None.
7. Select Show: Alphabetical List in the list box in the upper right corner of the Stylesheet editor.
8. Change the value of the Display property from list_item to block.
9. Save the revised style sheet.

That's it. Now to apply the style...

1. Type the list, including the continuation paragraphs to-be, select the entire list, and apply the desired numbered list style - Flare's default or your own.
2. Click on the continuation paragraph to-be, right-click on its structure bar, click on the Style Class option at the bottom of the menu, and click on the continuation style. This turns off the numbering of the continuation paragraph but keeps the indent and retains the proper numbering sequence for the next numbered item.

The images below illustrate the application process. The first image shows item 1 and a numbered item 2 that's meant to be the continuation paragraph for item 1. The list item numbers run from 1 to 4.

1. This is the first item in the numbered list.
2. This is some text that describes step 1 but is currently a numbered item. I want to turn off the numbering]
3. This is the second item in the list.
   This paragraph discusses the second list item. It has to have the same indent as the numbered item to which it refers, should not be numbered, and should not mess up the number sequence for the item that follows.
4. This is the third item in the list.

The next image shows a right-click on the li structure bar for item 2 and clicking of the Style Class option at the bottom. of the list. We'll assume that I had earlier created the continuation style called Number_1_continued.

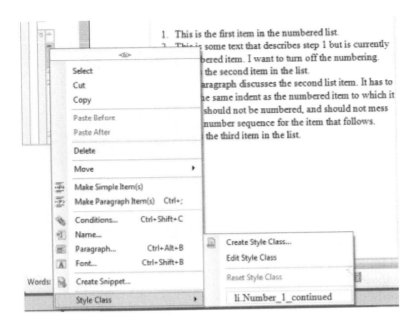

The next image shows the result of clicking the
Number_1_continued style.

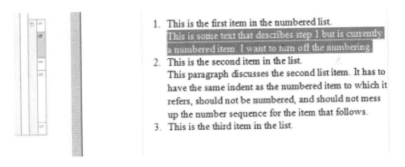

Numbered item 2 has now been turned into an unnumbered
continuation paragraph under item 1, and items 3 and 4
have been renumbered as 2 and 3, keeping the correct
numbering sequence.

If you're not used to working with styles beyond the basic head styles, it may take you a little while to get used to this new approach. But it is the best way to create your tables.

Adding a "Real" ToC and Index to PDF Output

Applies to versions 8, 9, and 10, with a new option in 10.

It's easy to output a Flare project as a PDF file. At a minimum, all you do is create a PDF target and generate it. The result looks like the example below:

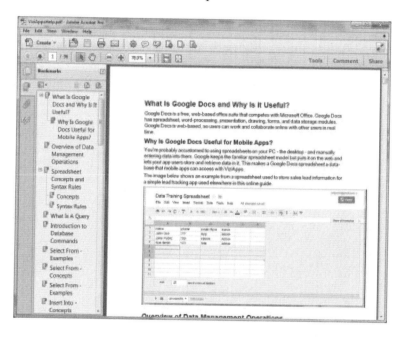

The content in this output begins on page 1; there's no title page or table of contents (ToC). What seems to be a ToC in the pane on the left is actually the list of bookmarks. It works, but it doesn't look like a real ToC, doesn't have page numbers, and won't print when you print the PDF. That may be okay if you're creating the PDF to send out for review comments but not if you're creating the PDF for distribution to users. In the latter case, how do you create a "real" ToC, one that's in in the body, has page numbers, and prints when you print the PDF? The answer applies to the index and various "tables of…", such as a table of figures, also. The process seems a little odd but works very well.

Step one is to create a topic to hold the print ToC. To do so, just create a new topic but select the TopicforTOC.htm template in the list of Factory Templates. Give this topic a name that defines its purpose, such as "printTOC". When the topic opens, you'll see this:

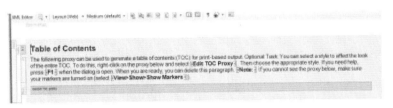

The paragraph of text is just a prompt. Delete it before creating the output. The important part is the proxy – the gray bar. (If you don't see the bar, select the Show Markers option.) When you generate the output, Flare takes the entries from the usual ToC and inserts them in this proxy.

Step two is to insert the ToC topic in the "real" ToC. Prior to this step, the "real" ToC, in the TOC Editor, looks like this:

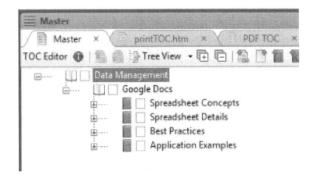

After inserting the ToC topic, by dragging it into the TOC Editor like any other topic, the "real" ToC looks like this:

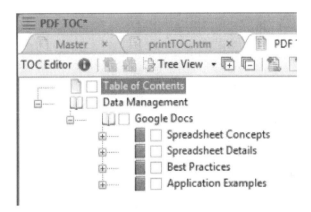

That "Table of Contents" entry, which belongs in the first position on the TOC Editor (except perhaps for a title page topic), takes the heading and topic listings in the rest of the ToC and lists them, with page numbers, as follows:

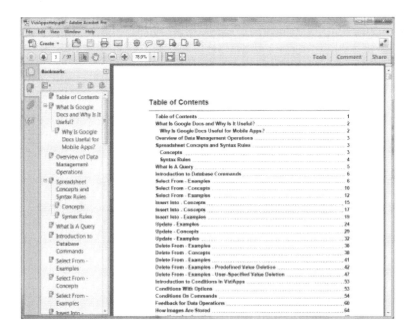

The process for adding a print index is similar. You'd still create a new topic, this time called something like "printIndex", and base it on the TopicforIndex.htm template in the Factory Templates list. The resulting topic will look like this:

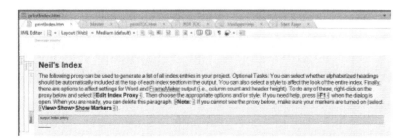

As with the printTOC topic, the paragraph of text is just a prompt that you delete. The proxy, the gray bar, is where the index entries appear – alphabetized and with page numbers. You can also modify the index settings by right-clicking on the proxy and selecting Edit Index Proxy, which displays the dialog box below where you can set properties like number of columns or whether to generate headings.

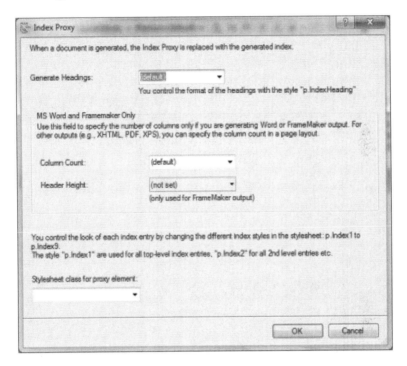

The last step is to add the printIndex topic to the ToC but at the bottom, in order to put the index at the end of the PDF like any traditional A-Z index you'd find in the back of a book. Like this:

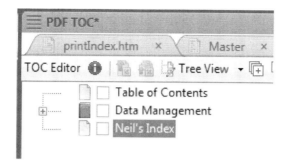

The result looks like this in PDF:

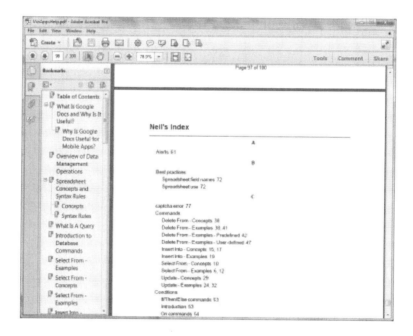

The steps are similar for adding lists of tables, images, and more – create a new topic based on the appropriate template, such as TopicForListOfImages.htm, set whatever parameters the proxy offers, and insert it in the desired position in the ToC on the TOC Editor.

What do you do if you need two different tables of contents for the online output and the print/PDF output? Either create two ToCs or create one that contains all the proxy topics and assign conditions to them, such as assigning a "Print" condition to the ToC and Index in order to exclude them when generating online output. You'll still get the ToC and index if you do that, but they'll be in the Contents and Index panes of the online output rather than inline in the body of the output.

In Flare 10 - Auto-Generated Print Proxies

The method described up to this point works perfectly, but users often view it as cumbersome and counterintuitive. In response, MadCap added a new, automated way to insert the TOC, Index, and Glossary proxies for print output in Flare 10. The old way is still available and still works fine, but the simplicity of the new way may lead many users to switch to it.

To use the new feature, open the Target Editor for the print-based target, open the Advanced tab, and select the desired proxies from the list in the Output Options group at the top of the Advanced tab, as shown below for the PDF Target Editor. That's it.

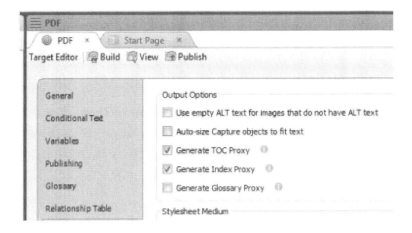

Flare automatically puts the TOC proxy at the top of the output or immediately after any title page. It automatically puts the Index proxy at the bottom of the output if the output contains any index entries. Finally, it automatically adds the Glossary proxy above the Index, if any.

The automatically added default proxies are plain. For example, here's the TOC in a tiny test output.

You can edit the proxies' headings and other properties. To edit the headings, see the Changing the Heading Text for Auto-Generated Proxies topic in the help. To edit the settings for the ToC, Index, or Glossary, see the Using Styles to Determine the Look of a Print TOC, Determining the Look of Your Print Index, or Using Styles to Change the Look of a Glossary topics in the help.

Change the Width of the Index Marker Field

Applies to versions 8, 9, and 10.

When you add index entries to topics, Flare shows the entries in a green box. In some cases, Flare won't show the full entry, just a portion of the entry followed by an ellipsis as shown below.

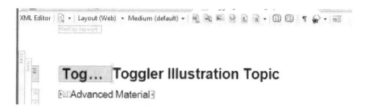

Technically, this is fine but it's hard to read. To fix it, widen the field. To do so, click the pulldown on the Show Tags icon on the upper XML Editor toolbar.

Then change the Marker Width at the bottom of the pulldown, shown below, to a wider setting. I use 800, but any width is okay.

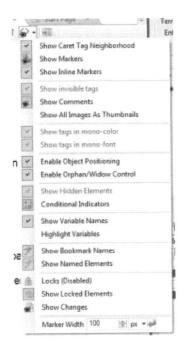

After typing the new width, click the blue arrow to the right of the Marker Width field to register your change. Here's the result of changing the width from 100 to 800.

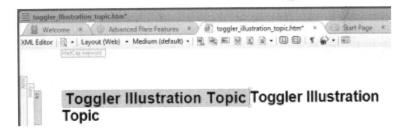

Word Import – Effect of Source Styles Options on Stylesheet Tab

Applies to versions 8, 9, and 10.

When you use the Word Import Editor to import or reimport Word documents into Flare, there are two options in the Stylesheet tab's Source Styles group (shown below) – Preserve MS Word Styles and Don't Preserve MS Word Styles – whose purposes aren't clear and whose results can be confusing.

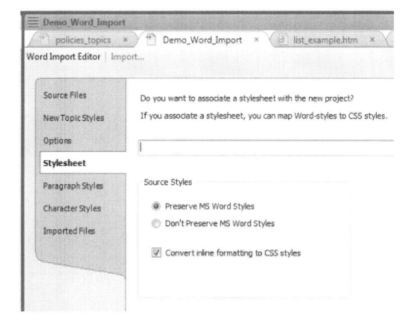

The Preserve… option keeps paragraph or character styles from the incoming Word document and appends their names to those of the Flare styles to which they're mapped.

(Mapping associates a CSS style to a Word style.) For example, if the Word document has a heading style called "MainHead," mapping it to Flare's "h1" style creates a combined style in Flare called "h1.MainHead"

Selecting the Don't Preserve… option tells Flare to not keep and append the Word style name to the mapped Flare style. So if a Word document uses a heading style called "MainHead" and you map this to Flare's "h1" style, Flare simply calls the style h1.

Why use the Preserve… option? It creates an historical record of style equivalence between the topics in Flare and the original Word document. For example, if you open a topic in Flare and see that its title style is "h1.MainHead", that tells you what the old Word title style was. If you need to know.

Why use the Don't Preserve… option? It avoids two peculiarities of the Preserve… option.

- Preserve… creates odd and potentially confusing styles like "h1.MainHead".
- Preserve… adds a confusing difference to the title styles in topics created in Flare and those created by importing a Word document. Topics created in Flare automatically use "h1" style for the title. But topics created in the same project by importing a document and with the Preserve… option selected automatically use "h1.<oldstyle>", like "h1.MainHead". When you or your successor reviews the project, you'll see what appear to be two inconsistent styles for topic titles. If you know

why, you can change them to a consistent form – easy to do but just one more thing to worry about… Or you just may not know why and be afraid to change them.

Tip: I generally recommend to my clients that they use the Don't Preserve… option to ensure that all topics, whether created in Flare or by import, use the standard "h1" style for their titles

Word Import – Split Long Topics Option on Options Tab

Applies to versions 8, 9, and 10.

Topics in Flare projects and Word documents are at the opposite ends of the length scale. Topics are as short as possible to make them readable and focused on one subject. A Word document is the opposite, almost a collection of topics. So you want to break a long Word document into a set of smaller topics when importing the document into Flare.

You can do this with multiple cut-and-pastes – create a new topic, cut some material out of the Word document and paste it in the new topic, and repeat until you've broken the document into topics. This works, but it's tedious and time-consuming.

A better, and automatic, way to do this is to have Flare break the document into topics at each head style when you import it. Flare will scan the document and indicate that it contains, for example, heads 1, 2, and 3. You might then tell Flare to split the document on head 1 and head 2. Every time Flare finds a head 1 or 2, it starts a new topic there and continues that topic until it finds the next head 1 or 2. If it finds a head 3, it makes that section part of the head 2 above it because you didn't tell Flare to break the document at a head 3. It's neat, simple, and quick, with one exception.

The exception is a document whose author used local formatting rather than styles to format the headings. In this case, you can't use the break-on-head-style method because there are no head styles. Instead, you can break the document at arbitrary points based on character count, such as telling Flare to start a new topic every 10,100th character. That's the purpose of the Split Long Topics features on the Options tab on the Word Import editor, shown below.

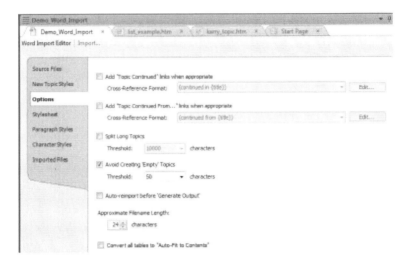

The "threshold" value sort of tells Flare the character number at which to split the incoming document – e.g. split it and create a new topic at character 10,001. However, Flare doesn't literally do this since that might create one topic with 10,000 characters and one with 1 character or split a document in the middle of a word. Instead, Flare will split the document at the paragraph closest to character 10,001. So this feature doesn't give results that are quite as arbitrary as they initially seem.

However, the problem is that you still can't be sure where Flare will split the incoming document. A better approach is to open the Word document before importing it into

Flare, apply head styles to the headings, then import the document by splitting it on those head styles.

Tip: Don't use both features – split on head styles and split on a length threshold – because it's impossible to predict what results you'll get.

Word Import – Avoid Creating Empty Topics Option on Options Tab

Applies to versions 8, 9, and 10.

The Word Import Editor's Options tab offers the "Avoid Creating 'Empty' Topics" feature. What's an "empty topic", why shouldn't you create one, and how does this feature work?

An empty topic results from importing a Word document containing a "naked" head into Flare. A naked head is one with no contents of its own and that's immediately followed by the next level of "real" head with contents, like the example in the image below.

This is a Level 1 Head

This is a Level 2 Head
And this is some text after a level 2 head.

This is Another Level 2 Head
And this is some text after a level 2 head.

The level 1 head has no content. It's simply a container for the level 2 heads that follow it and contain the real content. This is common in hard-copy writing and harmless until you import that document into Flare and tell Flare to split it on head styles, here head styles 1 and 2.

The result is normally three topics – the two level 2's with content and the empty level 1. The empty topic is a problem; you either have to delete it, and possibly change all your head 2s to head 1 to account for the now-deleted level 1 topic that contained them, or keep the level 1 topic but add artificial content to it. That's where Flare's "Avoid Creating 'Empty' Topics" option comes in.

The "Avoid Creating 'Empty' Topics" option lets you tell Flare the minimum number of characters that must be under a heading in order for that heading to be made a topic of its own on import, as opposed to being combined with the topic before or after it.

For example, if you import the document shown above, tell Flare to split it on head 1 and 2, and leave the "Avoid Creating…" option value set to 50, you'll get two topics. One will look like the image below, from the import preview window, and is what you'd expect.

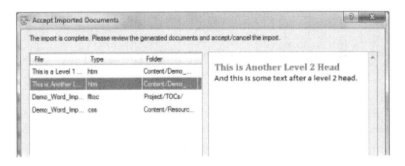

But the image below shows how the level 1 head topic comes in.

The threshold is 50 characters to avoid creating an empty topic. The level 1 head topic has fewer than 50 – it has 0 – and thus can't be brought in as a separate topic. It's combined with the topic after it. This is technically correct but annoying from a workflow standpoint. What do you do with that empty head 1?

If you add 50 characters of text under the head 1, the imported result looks like the example below.

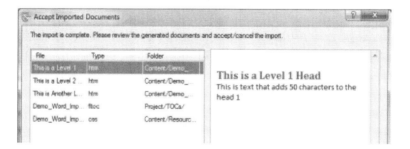

The head 1 now has enough text as to no longer be "empty" according to Flare and can be turned into a topic of its own.

So the "Avoid Creating 'Empty' Topics" option prevents Flare from creating empty topics when importing a Word document. But it's cumbersome to use with large documents because you have to check the content of each level 1 head to see how many characters it contains in order to determine the minimum threshold value to enter for the "Avoid Creating 'Empty' Topics" option. You don't want to set a value of 50, for example, only to discover that one of your level 1 heads only contains 49 and thus gets attached to the next head as in the second example above.

A better long run solution is to revise how you create documents in order to avoid using naked level 1 heads at all. However, this may be one of those things that you get to when you have time, which often means never. A short term solution may be to just set the "Avoid Creating 'Empty' Topics" option threshold value to 0 and clean up any empty topics that result. It's not the best solution but it may be the most realistic.

Word Import – Auto-Reimport Option on Options Tab

Applies to versions 8, 9, and 10.

If you connect your Flare project to a Word document by using the "Link Generated Files to Source Files" option on the Source Files tab of the Word Import Editor, you'll probably want to get any changes to the source Word document reflected in the topics in the Flare project. There are three ways to do this:

- Copy and paste manually – Open the Word document, copy the changed material, open the corresponding topic in Flare, and replace the original material with the new material that you copied from the Word document.
  This method is inefficient and tedious compared to the automated methods that Flare offers, but if you just have a few small changes to make (you have to define what "few" and "small" mean), this method may be the simplest and fastest because you're not spending time defining an import process for a one-time task. But if the changes are not few, small, or rare, then there are two better choices.
- Re-import manually – After you created the Flare Word import control file for the initial import, simply re-open that import control file and click the Re-import button at the top of the window.
  This method is simple. You simply have to know that the source Word document has changed and thus that you have to re-import it. This sounds

obvious, but it may not be if you don't own the source document and the person who does modifies it and forgets to tell you.

- Re-import automatically - After you created the import control file for the initial import and selected the "Link Generated Files to Source Files" option, there's nothing else for you to do. When you generate the output, Flare will compare the file creation date and time of the topics created from the initial Word import to the current file date and time of the source Word document. If the latter is newer, it means something in the source document has changed. Flare will automatically reimport the document and create new versions of the topics, over-writing any topics created from the prior import.
  This method is simple. Flare does it all – detects that the source Word document has changed and automatically reimports and splits it into topics for you. That ease makes this method a good choice.

However, both re-import methods have two issues to beware of.

- They put all the topics in a folder on the Content Explorer that has the same name as the import control file. For example, if you name the import control file Word_Import, Flare creates a folder by that name on the Content Explorer and puts all topics created by the import in that folder.

  However, if you import a Word document, move all topics created by the import into other folders on the Content Explorer, then re-import the Word document, you'll wind up with two versions of the same topics, one in the other folders and one in the import folder. It's not hard to figure out which ones are the right ones but it takes time.

- They overwrite any topics created from a previous import of the same Word document. If you did anything to those topics after the import, such as adding index entries or links or conditional build tags, you'll lose those changes when you re-import the Word document.

  Note: Do you need to apply conditional build tags to the topics created by importing a Word (or Framemaker) document but are concerned that you might have to reimport the document, which will overwrite the build tags? The solution is to apply the build tags to the folder that will contain the topics rather than to the topics themselves. This way, the topics will not be tagged but their "container" will be, which provides similar results when you use the conditionality to configure your single source outputs.

The solutions to both issues are simple, just requiring discipline. Leave the topics created from the import in the import folder and do not modify them in Flare unless you're absolutely certain that the source Word document won't change and thus won't require a re-import.

Context-Sensitive Help

Applies to versions 8, 9, and 10.

Context-sensitive help, or CSH, refers to online help that "knows" the user's location in a program, such as a dialog box, when the user asks for help and automatically opens the appropriate help topic rather than simply opening the help to the title page and leaving it up to the user to find the appropriate topic.

You can implement CSH in various ways depending on whether your programmers want to do it "their way" or are willing to use a standard method that's supported by Flare but may be new to them. Flare actually supports two ways to set up CSH. One is a formal method that's existed for almost 20 years and is well documented in the Flare help. The other is sort of a shortcut and less clearly documented in the Flare help but surprisingly simple. This section briefly touches on the formal method (because there's an excellent description of it in the Flare help), then focuses on the shortcut.

The goal of CSH is to find and display a topic containing information relevant to the user's location in the actual program. A topic is an HTM file so there's an easy way to create CSH – add a Help button in the program that, when clicked, follows a URL that opens the relevant HTM file in a single-pane window, like the one shown below.

If all the relevant information is in that one HTM file, then that link is all the programmers need to create. You just write the topics in Flare, or any HTML editor, and give them to the programmers.

Things get more complex when you decide to give users access to additional navigation features to let them explore on their own if the initial topic doesn't provide enough information. Those additional navigation features include the table of contents tab, index tab, search tab, and perhaps the favorites and glossary tabs. In other words, rather than the single pane help shown above, you want to provide the tri-pane, as shown below.

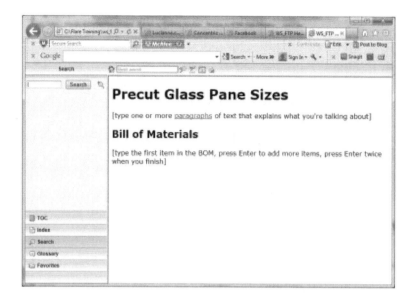

It's the same topic as the single pane help, but there are more navigation features in the form of the TOC, Index, and other tabs in the lower left. The question is how to get this look.

The Formal Road to CSH

The formal way to do so is to use the header-and-alias file model that's been used for years. (If you're coming from RoboHelp, the header file was called a map file.) This model uses a header file, which usually has an extension of .h, and an alias file, which has an extension of .ali, to connect the screen in the program to the help topic and display that topic when the user clicks the Help button or presses the F1 key. The Flare help does an excellent job of describing how this feature works and, rather than repeat the discussion, I'll recommend that you read the help topic called "About Context-Sensitive Help." It explains the concepts, some of the design issues, and the steps to perform depending on whether you or the programmer provides the core information.

The problem with the formal approach, from the programmers' perspective, is that they have to do most of the work. You use Flare to write the topics but the programmers have to do the coding within the "real" program to connect the help topics to the program. If this is an issue, the shortcut approach may be better.

The Shortcut to CSH

Unlike the formal approach to CSH, which opens the help in the tri-pane window automatically, the shortcut does not. Instead, when users access a help topic, it opens in single-pane mode but with a link that opens the tri-pane. The help topic below is open in single pane mode, but notice the links at the top and bottom of the topic – Open Topic With Navigation.

Clicking either link opens the tri-pane, with the navigation tabs on the left as shown below.

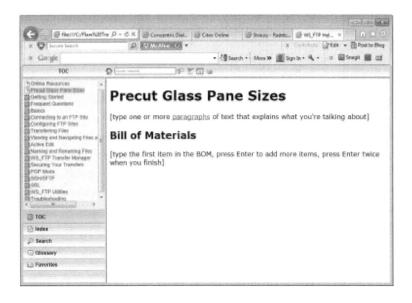

This approach requires no effort on the programmer's part other than adding a link from a Help button in the program to the help topic. The work of opening the navigation tabs is manual, done by the users. And it's easy to implement in Flare. All you have to do is open the WebHelp Setup tab on the WebHelp Skin Editor, or the Setup tab on the HTML5 Skin Editor (both shown below), and select either or both of the Show Navigation Link… options in the Topic Settings group at or near the bottom of the tab.

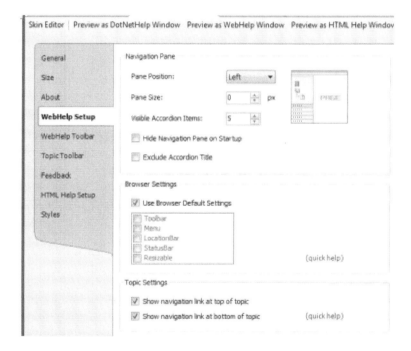

WebHelp Skin Editor - WebHelp Setup Tab

HTML5 Skin Editor - Setup Tab

Three things to be aware of with this feature:

- If you open a topic that has an Open Topic With Navigation link in IE, you will not see the links until you click the Allow Blocked Content option.
- During development, you'll only see the Open Topic With Navigation link in topics opened from

the Output folder, not the Project folder. Remember this if you do a demo for a client because the shortcut link will not work, in fact won't even be visible, if you try to demo the shortcut from topics in the Project folder.

- To change the wording of the link for WebHelp, open the Skin Editor, select the Styles tab, expand the Control group in the Styles list, select the NavigationLinkBottom or NavigationLinkTop option, expand the General group under Properties on the right side of the tab, and type the new label wording there.
For HTML5, open the Skin Editor, select the Styles tab, and expand Navigation Link under the Navigation group to change the font properties or select the UI Text tab and scroll down to Navigation Link.Bottom or Navigation Link.Top to change the wording.

WebHelp AIR

Applies to versions 8, 9, and 10.

AIR (Adobe Integrated Runtime) is an output format from Adobe that's a hybrid of browser-based and desktop applications. First released in 2008, it represents Adobe's attempt to get the best of both the web and local worlds. AIR is not specific to help; Adobe is implementing AIR across many of its product lines. But this discussion looks at AIR from the perspective of online help. (Although it's an Adobe format, other help vendors, like MadCap, have added support for it.)

As noted above, AIR is a hybrid of a browser-based application like WebHelp, and a desktop application like the Microsoft HTML Help .chm format. A little history to put this statement, and AIR, in context...

In the late 1980s, Microsoft released Windows Help ("WinHelp"), the first mainstream online help format. WinHelp was "compiled". This combined all the topics in an online help output in one file, the .hlp, for distribution. (A second file, the .cnt, controlled the table of contents. We can ignore it here.) No matter whether you had 1 topic or 1,000 in your help, they were distributed as one HLP file. This one-file model made WinHelp easy to distribute.

In 1997, Microsoft released WinHelp's successor, HTML Help. It too was compiled into and distributed as one file, the .chm. (No cnt file this time.) As with WinHelp, the one-file model made the HTML Help easy to distribute. But this time, Microsoft got tripped up by the spread of networks in general, the web in particular.

HTML Help wasn't designed for a web-based or non-Microsoft world. It could only run on Windows PCs with IE, and could only run locally or off a network drive. As more people began turning to the web and as other platforms like Linux began to take off, HTML Help began hitting its limits. This happened quickly - as early as mid-1997 people were complaining about the format's Microsoft-centricity.

In early 1998, eHelp came out with a solution – WebHelp. (eHelp was the renamed Blue Sky Software, the original maker of RoboHelp and later acquired by Macromedia, then Adobe.) WebHelp looked similar to HTML Help but had two major differences. It was browser-based and it didn't bundle the topics into one distributable file like the chm. Instead, WebHelp kept the topics as individual files managed by various control files. In effect, WebHelp was a web site with a help-like interface. This added great flexibility. WebHelp could run on almost any platform (Windows, Mac, UNIX, etc.) and browser and from any location (local, network drive, or server).

But WebHelp wasn't perfect. It wasn't compiled, so the output had as many files as the number of topics, graphics, and control files. A 1000-topic WebHelp system might have 1500 files – topics, graphics, control files, etc.- which made engineering and network management unhappy. ("Fifteen-hundred files! For a help system!?") Plus WebHelp adds work for the vendors since it has to be tested under and reconciled for different browsers and new versions of existing browsers.

So the ideal solution would be an output format that could run locally in order to reduce network traffic, went back to the one-file model of WinHelp and HTML Help in order to simplify distribution, got away from the browser compatibility testing problem, and was network aware… AIR.

If you output a help project to AIR, the AIR "packager" bundles the topics, graphics, and control files into one file with an air extension that runs locally, on the user's C drive. It also avoids the browser compatibility problem by using its own viewer. (More on that below.) It's network-aware to handle updates. It has WebHelp-style attributes like the ability to use skins to customize the interface. It lets you create links to external targets like web pages and can run them in separate windows. Plus, because it's running locally, it can take advantage of local features like file writes. For example…

The screen below shows a simple WebHelp project created in Flare 8. It has the usual tri-pane features, and some formatting,

The next screen shows the same project output to AIR with no formatting changes – just a simple conversion. It keeps the tri-pane look but lost the formatting, which can easily be reapplied. There are other, AIR-specific features that you can add but the basic AIR looks very similar to the WebHelp.

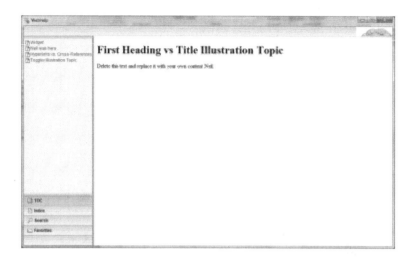

So output to AIR will call for some tweaking but not too much.

On the minus side, several things to consider:

AIR requires that authors (not viewers) have the Sun JRE (Java RunTime Environment) on their PCs. This isn't a big deal but it's an unusual configuration step and Sun's download page can be confusing.

AIR's use of a proprietary viewer instead of a browser isn't a big deal unless you support a "zero-footprint" environment in which viewers can't download anything to their PCs. That means they won't be able to download the viewer and thus can't view the AIR Help. (This is a problem today, but history suggests that it may become less of one. In 1997, WebHelp developers couldn't be sure that viewers had any browser; today, it's taken for granted. In 1999, developers couldn't be sure that viewers would have the Flash Player; today, Adobe claims that 99% of all web-capable PCs have it. The AIR viewer is the latest in the "we're not sure if users have it…" category but, if AIR takes off, the viewer may turn into one more default feature on users' PCs.)

AIR's ability to use local PC features like writing to the hard disk can be a security risk. Adobe is dealing with this by requiring that developers create digital certificates for their AIR applications. It should solve the problem, but my experience is that this still can make network administrators nervous.

In my experience – yours may differ – these problems offset the AIR benefits and have consigned it to niche status in the help world. But if you need the one-file distribution model, plus network awareness for automatic updating, it's worth a look. You can find Flare-specific information about it in the About WebHelp AIR Output topic in the Flare help, and more information about it in general at the Adobe AIR Developer Center at http://www.adobe.com/devnet/air.html and on Wikipedia at http://en.wikipedia.org/wiki/Adobe_Integrated_Runtime

Master Project (Flare Project Import) Considerations

Applies to versions 8, 9, and 10.

Will you ever have to use similar settings or files in multiple projects, whether they're being created by one author or several authors? For example, requiring that all projects use the same styles, list the same copyrights and permissions, use the same logo, etc?

This need for consistency seems straightforward, but implementing it can be difficult. For example, one common approach to creating a standard format is to create a standard CSS and send it to all authors to add to their projects. But do you trust all the authors to do so? Can you trust that they won't tweak a setting just a bit?

Things get worse if you have to modify a CSS and get all authors to use the new version. You again have to distribute the CSS to all the authors, get them to install it in the right place, and use it without modifying it. The master project feature (officially the Flare Project Import feature) offers a solution.

Once you designate a project as the master project, all authors can use specific files from the master project in their individual projects. They do this by linking their projects to the master and specifying the files from the master to use in their projects. This means the master project is acting like a control file repository – a central master set of control files.

The obvious question is whether authors can modify the control files from the master project after copying them to their projects. If so, doesn't that negate the centralized control aspect of the master project? This Flare feature is set up to eliminate that problem.

To use the master project approach, link your individual project to the master by using Flare's Project Import Editor, available from the Imports folder on the Project Organizer in the actual project, and shown below, or by selecting File > New and selecting Flare Import File from the File Type list at the top of the Add File dialog box.

The top field lets you select the project to use as the master. You can then specify which files to import (include) from the master to your project. You can also specify which files not to import – e.g. to specifically exclude. The choice between include and exclude depends on the number and types of files that you want to use; select include to use just a few files or one type from the master, or exclude to use all but a few files or types. You can also conditionalize the link to the master project.

The feature at the top, Auto-Reimport Before "Generate Output," tells Flare to always use the master file version of any linked file. For example, if you link to a CSS in the master project and then modify the copy of that CSS in your project, Flare will recopy the CSS from the master project to your project when you generate your output. This forces consistency; any changes you made to the CSS are overwritten by the master CSS. This also helps the lead writer enforce format consistency; no matter what changes you make to the CSS in your project, the master CSS takes precedence. This means that any changes to that master CSS by its owner will always take effect.

The master project feature has two design considerations:

- Keep it simple and easy to understand.
  Flare lets you create master projects two ways. You can create a "real" master whose purpose is to hold the files to be linked to other projects. Or you can turn an existing project into the master. The second option is easier in the short run because the project already exists. You're just using it for an extra purpose – e.g. it's still a real project of its own,

you're just using it as a master project too. But the first option is better in the long run because its sole purpose is to be the master project. It won't have the extraneous files and topics of the "real" project that can be confusing when the time comes to maintain the master project or even to simply link to it.

- Make sure it has a designated owner.
  A common problem with any multi-project material is that because it belongs to multiple projects, it doesn't belong to any one and thus no one owns it. That means that it and the logic behind it may get forgotten, so that projects suddenly start to misbehave for no apparent reason. I've seen several instances where an actual project linked to a master project and used the CSS from the master but the link from the project to the master was broken. This meant that the format of the actual project was wrong. Flare was showing that the link to the master was broken in the error list on the Generate dialog box but the author didn't realize what that error meant. Similarly, I've seen an instance where the original "owner" of the master project had left the company and no one had taken over responsibility for the master project. The result was that individual project authors would modify their project CSSs only to have their changes overwritten by the CSS from the master project but not understand why and assume that Flare had gotten corrupted somehow.

In summary, the master project feature is very useful but, due to its cross-project effect, has to be actively owned and managed.

Apply One or More CSSs to a Project

Applies to versions 8, 9, and 10.

Most projects use a single regular CSS (ignoring table CSSs, of which a project can use one or more in addition to the regular CSS). Why might you want to use more than one regular CSS in a project, and how do you apply them to your project?

The only reason *I've* found for using multiple CSSs in a project is if a help system is to include topics from different modules of a project and you want to visually distinguish the different topics. In that case, you might apply CSS A to the first hundred topics and CSS B to the next hundred. This works but has two drawbacks.

- You have to remember which CSS to apply to which topics.
- You have to remember to apply that CSS when you create a new topic, either in Flare or by import from Word, Framemaker, or some other authoring tool.

If you do want to apply different CSSs to different topics, there are several ways to do so.

- Apply the CSS as you create a new topic, one at a time directly in Flare, by selecting it in the Stylesheet field on the new topic dialog box, shown below.

- Apply the CSS by selecting it in the Stylesheet field on the Import Editor, shown below, when you create new topics by importing Word or Framemaker files.

- Apply the CSS to multiple topics by multi-selecting those topics in the File List (opened by selecting the View menu item and File List on the left side of the ribbon), then opening the Properties pane and selecting the desired CSS, then repeating for the next set of topics.

These approaches are flexible but have the same problem – you have to remember to apply the CSS. A better approach is to set a CSS as a master stylesheet for the project. This automatically applies that CSS to every topic in the project and to every new topic, whether created directly in Flare or by importing a Word or Framemaker file. This effectively creates an "invisible" standard. To do so, open the Project Properties dialog box and specify the master CSS in the Master Stylesheet field on the Defaults tab. The only drawback to using a master CSS is that you can only have one CSS applied to the project. In most cases, however, this isn't a drawback since most projects use one CSS anyway.

Popups – Topic vs. Text – Design Considerations

Applies to versions 8, 9, and 10.

Most Flare authors who use popups use topic popups but there is another type called a text popup. The two look similar; they show their contents in a window that "pops up" on top of the current topic. The image below shows a topic popup.

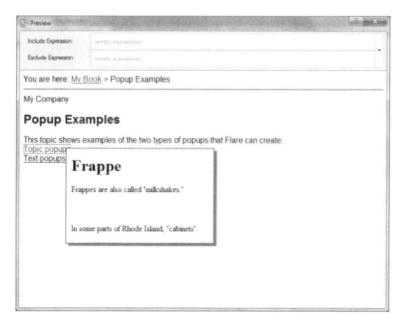

Clicking the hotspot, the words "Topic popup", opens a window on top of the current topic. The window has a box border and a drop shadow on the right side and the bottom.

The image below shows a text popup.

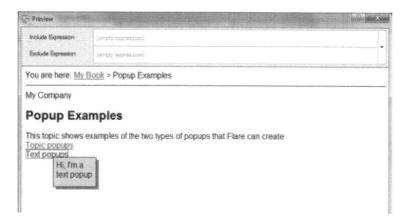

Clicking the hotspot, the words "Text popup", opens a window on top of the current topic. It too has a box border and drop shadow on the right side and bottom and, except for the gray background and size, looks like the topic popup. But the two are different.

A topic popup is like a regular hyperlink to a target topic, except that the user sees the target topic in a window that "pops up" on top of the current window rather than jumping to the target topic. This means that a topic popup can display anything you'd put in a topic – text, plus graphics, tables, links, etc. It also means that you might create fifty topic popup links to one topic, tech support contact information for example, but you'd only have to change the information in the one topic if the phone number changes.

A text popup doesn't display the content of a topic; it only shows text. And the text that displays in the popup window is physically embedded in the topic that contains the text popup. You can see this in the image below, where the text that pops up is part of the topic, on line 12.

```
     popup_examples.htm
   popup_examples.htm  ×     popup_examples.htm  ×     toggler_slustration_topic.htm  ×     1st_headi
Text Editor
1      <?xml version="1.0" encoding="utf-8"?>
2    <html xmlns:MadCap="http://www.madcapsoftware.com/Schemas/MadCap.xsd" MadCap:la
3       <head>
4       </head>
5       <body>
6          <h1>Popup Examples</h1>
7          <p>This topic shows examples of the two types of popups that Flare can
8          <p><a href="frappe.htm" target="_popup" class="Popup">Topic popups</a>
9          <p>
10             <MadCap:popup>
11                <MadCap:popupHead>Text popups</MadCap:popupHead>
12                <MadCap:popupBody>Hi, I'm a text popup</MadCap:popupBody>
13             </MadCap:popup>
14          </p>
15       </body>
```

Why does the difference matter? Say you create ten text popups that list a contact phone number and the number changes. You have to find and change all ten instances. (You might be able to use a snippet instead, but that's a more complex solution than simply using the topic-type popup.) Because of the maintenance difficulty, I usually recommend topic popups over text popups.

Slideshows

Applies to versions 10.

The slideshow feature is conceptually simple – a set of horizontal slides containing images or other types of content including, from the Flare help, "…snippets, text, tables, and more…" in a topic. The slides, from the help, are "useful for showing a gallery of images or videos…" Users can move between slides using arrow buttons on either side of a slide or the "pager," the dots, beneath each slide. (You can replace the dots with thumbnail images).

To see an example, open the Flare 10 help's table of contents and select PDF Guides, the fifth option on the list. Here's the result.

You can navigate sequentially through the slides by clicking the left or right arrow buttons on either side of the slide, or sequentially or randomly by clicking the pager (the dots) beneath each slide. (The pager navigation is sequential if you click the dots in sequence, random if you click them out of sequence.)

Here's another example, three slides showing a series of cute dog photos and some explanatory text for each photo. Each slide has its own narration under the title "Cute Dog Picture..."

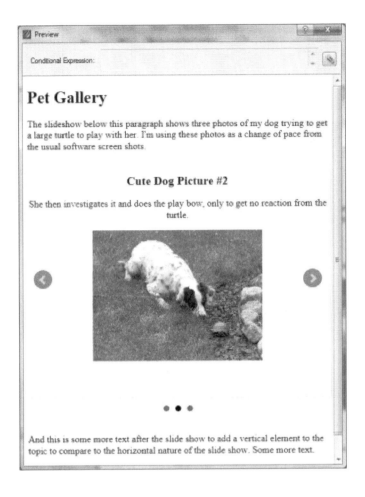

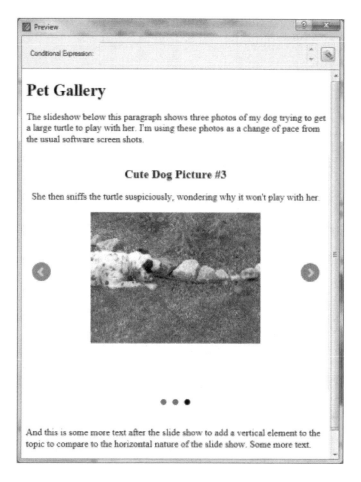

Notice two things about these three slides.

As noted earlier, you can navigate sequentially by clicking on the arrow buttons on either side of the slide. You can also navigate sequentially or randomly by clicking on the pager dots below each slide.

Notice that the position of the elevator box on the scroll bar hasn't changed in the three slides. You're staying in one place vertically and moving horizontally until you resume the vertical scrolling.

In addition to showing "a gallery of images" as the help states, the slideshow feature could solve an old design problem inherent in task description or procedure topics.

If you create topics containing numbered steps, it's good practice to not insert links that take users out of the list, or thread, of steps because that makes it easy for users to lose their place. This rules out using jump links/hyperlinks.

Authors typically use popups, dropdowns, or togglers instead, but each of these types of links has a drawback. Popups cover up part of the main topic and can only contain so much material. Dropdowns don't cover the main topic but can still only contain so much material before readers start to lose track of their position in the main topic. Togglers can have so many chunks of content popping up all over a topic that readers can again start to lose track of their vertical position.

The slideshow feature solves these problems. It lets authors add as much material as they need in as many slides as they need without changing readers' vertical position in the topic. In other words, readers get to a slideshow, view it horizontally, then continue reading vertically. This could be useful in task description topics that contain numbered steps but also contain long or complex side explanations.

Converting "Special" links When Outputting to Print

Applies to versions 8, 9, and 10.

Flare offers four "special" types of links in addition to the familiar hyperlink, or jump link:

- Popups
- Dropdowns
- Expanding ("slideout") links
- Togglers

For example, here's a closed dropdown in WebHelp format.

And here's that same link but open.

These links are designed for online targets like WebHelp; what happens if you output to print targets like Word or PDF?

Hyperlinks work as long as you view the document on the screen rather than on paper, but the special links don't. You can either not use the special links at all, or use them and use the link conversion features in the Advanced tab of the Target Editor for the print formats, shown in the image below.

- The "convert to footnotes" option, the default, literally converts the body text of the link to a numbered footnote.
- The "expand text inline" option displays the link and the body, as if you'd clicked the link to open it.
- The "remove the body" option hides the body and turns the link to ordinary text.

The "convert to footnotes" option seems to be the most useful because it lets you retain the body of the link that you thought was important enough to create in the first place.

Glossary Term Conversion Options on Target Editor's Glossary Tab

Applies to versions 8, 9, and 10.

If you need an online glossary, Flare makes it easy to add it as a part of the output interface. Just add the terms and definitions by using the Glossary Editor, shown in the image below.

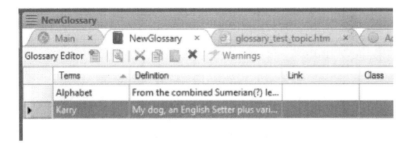

And select Glossary in the Features list on the General tab of the Skin Editor, shown in the next image, to turn it on.

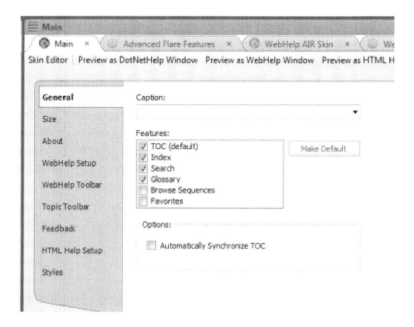

The result looks like the image below, WebHelp in this instance.

But there's another question to consider when you generate the output, the Glossary Term Conversion options on the Glossary tab of the Target Editor, shown in the next image.

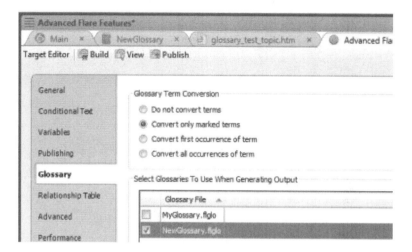

These options let you convert instances of terms on the Glossary tab into popup links in the output when those terms appear within a topic. Let's see what the options do. First, look at the image below, which shows several instances of the word "Karry" in the text, none of which is flagged as glossary entries. But the word "Karry" is a glossary entry on the Glossary tab.

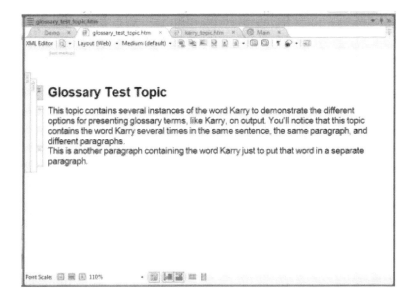

Here's the effect of each option on the output:

- Do not convert terms – Does not convert instances of a Glossary tab term in a topic to linked terms. Using the Glossary Test Topic above as an example, the result is as shown below. The word Karry in the Glossary tab is linked, but the words Karry in the topic remain as text in the output.

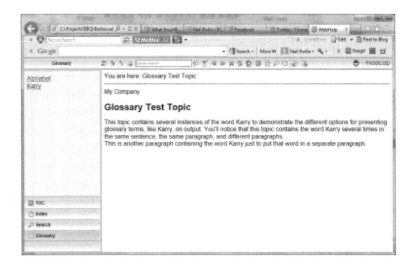

- Convert only marked terms – Only converts instances of a Glossary tab term in the topic to linked terms if they were inserted in the topic that way. If not, the terms in a topic remain as text. Using the Glossary Test Topic as an example, the result is as shown just above. The terms in the topic remain as text in the output.

The next two options let you automatically convert instances of a Glossary tab term that appear in a topic to actively linked terms.

- Convert first occurrence... – Converts the first instance of a Glossary tab term in a topic to a linked term, even if the instance was inserted as text. Other instances within a topic remain as text. Using the Glossary Test Topic as an example, the result is as shown below. The first word Karry in the topic is automatically linked to its definition in the form of a popup without your having to link it. The remaining instances of Karry remain text in the output.

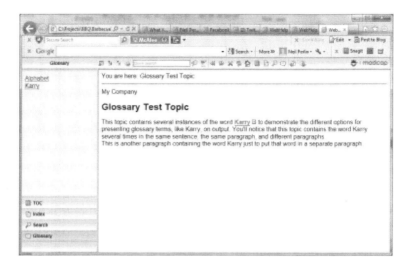

- Convert all occurrences... – Converts all instances of a Glossary tab term in a topic to linked terms, even if the instances were inserted as text. Using the Glossary Test Topic as an example, the result is as shown below. All instances of Karry are automatically linked to the definition in the form of a popup.

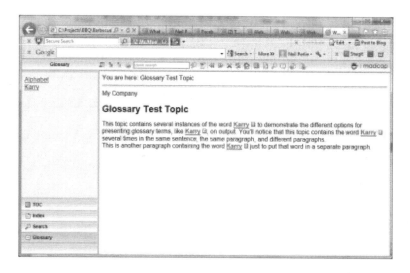

Many authors use the second, default, option or the first. What about the two automatic options?

One school of thought says to use the third option. This links the first instance of a term in the topic, so that readers see the link the first time they encounter it, at which point they might need a definition, but not after. Any more would be irritating. This is a valid argument as long as readers always enter a topic at the top.

However, if you use bookmarks as link targets, a reader might follow a link, enter the target topic at a bookmark below the first glossary definition, and encounter another instance of the glossary term that thus doesn't have the linked definition. This argues for using the "Convert all..." option. However, that option might create multiple instances of the same glossary term link in the same paragraph, which will probably annoy readers.

Because of this, my recommendation is to create a Glossary tab and use the first option so that all glossary terms are listed only on the Glossary tab and not within the bodies of the topics.

Glossary – Text vs Linked Definitions

Applies to versions 8, 9, and 10.

To create an online glossary, add the terms and definitions by using the Glossary Editor, shown in the image below.

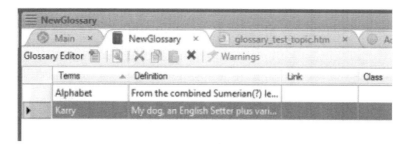

And select Glossary in the Features list on the General tab of the Skin Editor to turn it on. The result looks like the image below, in WebHelp in this case.

Making the glossary part of the navigation tab has two benefits.

- The glossary gets the same level of visual emphasis as the TOC, Index, and Search tabs.
- Users can find the definition of a word in the topic they're reading without having to jump to another topic that contains the definition, thus losing the thread. They can simply find the term in the glossary tab, find its definition, and go back to reading.

But creating a glossary tab like this has one problem. It can only show one paragraph of text and can't show:

- Multiple paragraphs.
- Bulleted or numbered lists.
- Graphics.
- Formatting.

- Links.

This makes the glossary tab good for terms with short definitions, like simple terms or acronym expansions, but not so good for more complex definitions.

If your glossary contains terms whose definitions require the unsupported features, you can instead create a Glossary *topic* that lists the terms, create a separate topic for each definition, which lets you include the unsupported features in the definition, then create topic popup links for each term in the Glossary topic to the appropriate definition topic. This works, but it's not as visually strong as a Glossary tab.

Some authors create both, a tab for simple terms and acronym expansions and a topic for the other terms. This works technically but can confuse users who don't understand the logic for having two separate glossaries.

Flare offers a partial solution by letting you create one Glossary tab that can show the definitions both ways, as dropdown links on the tab itself, shown in the image below.

Or as links to topics that contain those unsupported features, shown in the image below.

This dual option seems to solve the problem of having to create two separate glossaries, a tab for the simple terms and acronym expansions and a topic for the terms whose definitions require the images, etc. However, as usual, the answer isn't this clear.

Having a Glossary tab whose definitions appear either as dropdowns or as links means that users who click on a term won't know how the definitions will appear. This inconsistency can be annoying. It can also get readers lost because as they read a topic and look up a term in the Glossary tab, the topic they're reading might remain on the screen or might be replaced by the topic containing the definition and they won't know which to expect for any given glossary term. The moral – be consistent in how you present glossaries and glossary term definitions.

Mobile Outputs – ePub, WebHelp, WebHelp Mobile, HTML5

Applies to versions 8, 9, and 10, with some differences between the versions, discussed below.

"Mobile" is becoming a hot topic in technical communication and Flare supports several forms. In order to put the rest of this topic into context, here's an overview of mobile.

Note: You'll also want to factor responsive design into your thinking about mobile. (See "Responsive Design and the "Un-Desktop"" on page 205)

The term "mobile" refers to apps and ebooks. In brief:

- Native apps follow the rules of a particular platform. We refer to such apps by the platform name – e.g. iPhone apps, Android apps, etc. Native apps have two main benefits – speed, because they adhere to the platform standards, and simple access to "on-device resources" like the camera, GPS, and accelerometers.
  Native apps also have drawbacks. If your users have different devices, usually iPhones and Androids, or different versions of the same devices, such as different phones from different manufacturers that run different versions of Android, you may have to create a version of the app for each platform. It's an expensive job.

You also have to QA each platform or operating system, another expensive job.

- Web apps display in a browser on any device no matter what the platform. (This means that traditional WebHelp is effectively a web app – more on that below.) Web apps offset the benefits and drawbacks of native apps. You only need to create one, or a few, versions of the app since there are fewer browser variants than platform variants. However, web apps may be slower than native apps and don't provide easy access to the on-device resources. (It's harder to integrate a smartphone camera into a web app than into a native app.) Hybrid apps are a fairly recent development. They use the best of native apps and web apps to fix the problems.
- ebooks are basically books that are read on the screen.

Here are three ways to distinguish ebooks from apps:

- ebooks are usually read sequentially, like novels, while apps are usually read randomly, like an encyclopedia. This is good for sequential material, less so for highly chunked material like a help system.
- ebooks are usually read on devices like the Barnes & Noble Nook or the Amazon Kindle, but we can also read ebooks by loading ebook reader plug-ins on general purpose devices like smartphones or tablets. This variety makes it easy to get ebooks into readers' hands, but different devices or plug-ins may have

different levels of support for different ebook standards and features so the reading experience may not be consistent.

- ebooks usually reside *on* the reading device as opposed to apps, which may be on the device but may also be on a server. This is fine if the content is stable, but can be difficult to keep up to date if the content does change because there are likely to be older versions of the ebook on people's readers.

There are several ebook standards at this time, one of the main ones being ePub from the International Digital Publishing Forum (http://idpf.org/), which Flare supports for reading on a dedicated reader like the Barnes and Noble Nook or on a general-purpose device with an ePub plug-in. Note that Flare 9 and 10 can also generate another output format called mobi.

How do these choices affect Flare?

- ebooks – If you need to support ebooks, select ePub format for your target. Here's a project output to ePub with no changes at all:

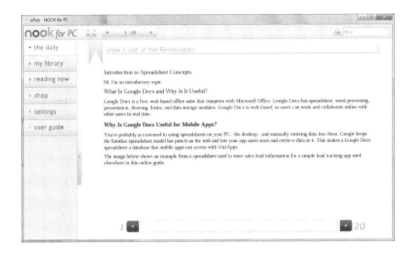

Some of the heading formatting needs to be corrected but, aside from that, the project converted fine.

- Web apps – You have two choices for web apps. One, mentioned earlier, is the traditional bowser-based WebHelp, which is *effectively* a web app. If users can open a browser window on their mobile device, they can display a WebHelp output. The problem with WebHelp is that it's not optimized for display on small screen devices, which means a lot of scrolling, pinching, and zooming. The alternative is to output to Flare's WebHelp Mobile format. It's basically the same as traditional WebHelp but with a skin that's optimized for the small, portrait formatted smartphones, as shown below. Or you can use HTML5 for your default output format and turn on the responsive design feature. (See "Responsive Design and the "Un-Desktop"" on page 205)
First, a traditional WebHelp output:

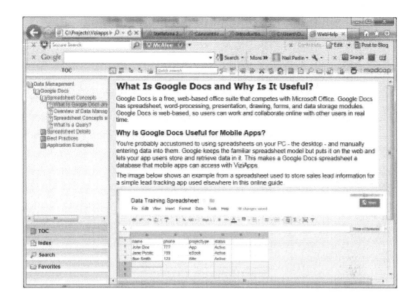

And here's the same project in WebHelp Mobile format:

- Native apps – Flare doesn't support native app output. However, Adobe's adding native app output (iPhone and Android) in RoboHelp 10 suggests that MadCap may look to add that in a future version of Flare.
- Hybrid apps – Flare doesn't support hybrid apps. But because HTML5 is one of the technologies at the base of a hybrid app, this suggests that with some extensions of the code and the addition of a viewer in a future version of Flare, the result could be support for hybrid.

Conditional Build Tags

Applies to versions 8, 9, and 10, with some changes in 9 and 10.

A condition is simply a category and a build tag is a marker for a category. You'd use conditions if you need to categorize material in a project in order to be able to selectively extract a subset of that material for particular outputs.

Let's say you create a project to generate an operations manual for two US and Canadian plants. Most of the material is the same for both plants but some differs, so you want the ability to exclude US-specific material from the Canadian output and vice versa. Without categorization, it's hard to selectively exclude any of the material because it's all tangled together. However, if you've categorized the material as US-only, Canadian-only, or Both, you can then tell Flare to exclude all material in the US-only category from the Canadian output and vice versa. That ability to categorize project elements and then manipulate them based on their category is the basic concept behind conditional build tagging.

Think of conditional build tag as filters and you have the concept.

Some Examples of Conditionality

You want to create one project that serves multiple markets, such as the US and Canadian markets, and include or exclude different material depending on the market. You might do this by creating and applying two build tags called US_only and Canadian_only and telling Flare to exclude any material that carries the appropriate tag when generating the output.

You want to create a project that can output to multiple devices. For example, you might output to online and print and have to be able to exclude print-only content from the online output and vice versa. Or you might output to large screen and mobile devices and need to be able to exclude certain graphics from the mobile output because they're too large for the screen and can't be shrunk without making them unreadable. You might do this by creating and applying a build tag called not_for_mobile and telling Flare to exclude any material that has the not_for_mobile tag when generating the mobile output.

You want to add developer notes as a topic of its own in a project but want to exclude that topic from the output. You might do this by creating and applying a build tag called developer_notes and telling Flare to exclude any material that has the developer_notes tag when generating the output.

You want to exclude unfinished topics from a build when sending it out for review so that reviewers don't see unfinished material. You might do this by creating and applying a build tag called in_progress and telling Flare to exclude any material that has the in_progress tag when generating the output.

Working With Conditional Build Tags

Working with conditional build tags is a four step process.

1. Set the goals. This crucial step is often overlooked because build tags are so easy to create and apply. But you'll see the problem when you generate the output and find that you're getting the wrong results because the build tags weren't thought out carefully in the first place.
2. Create the build tags.
3. Apply the tags to elements in a project. You can apply tags to one character in a topic, a paragraph of text, a topic, a folder-full of topics, and any other element with the build tag indicator (□) on the Content Explorer, Project Organizer, and TOC Editor. This flexibility makes Flare's conditionality feature extraordinarily powerful; you can even apply conditions to conditions! But it also makes it easy to lose track of what your conditions are supposed to do.
4. Preview the topic or generate the full output using the build tags by defining a condition tag expression (formula).

The Logic of Conditionality

The main problem people have with conditionality is that fact that Boolean logic is not the same as everyday logic. To explain why, here's some background followed by a little test.

After applying conditions, you can tell Flare to include or exclude conditionally tagged elements when you preview a topic or build the output. Any tagged element can be included or excluded. Any element that isn't tagged is always included.

Note: It's possible to apply two different tags to the same element and then accidentally tell Flare to include one tag and exclude the other. In this case, Flare defaults to including the element, but it can still be confusing figuring out what's going on.

Here's the test. There are eight topics listed below. Topics 1-4 have no build tags. Topics 5 and 6 have build tag A applied. Topics 6, 7, and 8 have build tag B applied.

1	2	3	4
5A	6AB	7B	8B

If we tell Flare to include build tag A, what topics do we get? The answer is 1, 2, 3, and 4 (they have no build tag, so they're always selected) plus 5 and 6 (which have build tag A applied).

If we tell it to include build tag B, what's the result? The answer is 1, 2, 3, and 4 (no build tag = always selected) plus 6, 7, and 8 (which have build tag B).

If we tell it to include build tag A and B, what's the result? People usually say 1-8, but the answer is really 1-4 plus 6 (the only topic with build tag A AND B). To get 1-8, we have to tell Flare to include build tag A OR B.

The problem, as noted earlier, is that Boolean logic isn't the same as everyday logic. This makes it easy to define build tags incorrectly.

Basic and Advanced Build Tagging

Logical stumbling blocks aside, build tagging was straightforward up through Flare 8 because the build tag options were limited to include or exclude, specified in the Build Tag dialog box, shown below.

The expression at the bottom of the dialog box includes build tag A which is in the Default Build Tag group. This basically adds an OR operator to the expression, whereas an exclude adds a NOT operator. For example, excluding tag B generates the expression NOT B. What if you want to create more complex expressions?

In Flare 9, MadCap added an Advanced feature to the dialog box. We can now use Basic mode, shown below, which looks just like the older version.

Or we can use Advanced mode, shown below.

Selecting the Advanced option in the left center of the dialog box hides the Basic view's Include/Exclude options and lets us type more complex expressions. For example, selecting two conditions to include in Basic view is equivalent to an OR, as shown below.

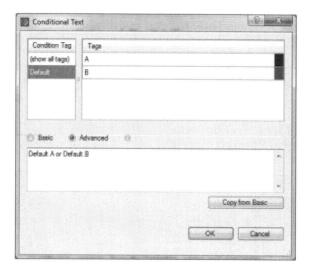

How do we add an AND expression? We simply add the first tag to the text box, then type an AND and the next tag. For example:

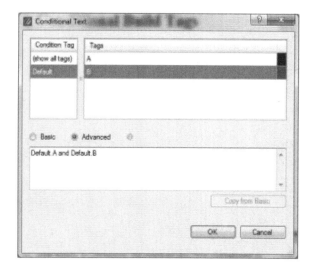

Five observations about working in the Flare 9 (and 10) build expression dialog box's Advanced mode.

1. If you select Include/Exclude options while in Basic mode and then switch to Advanced mode, click the Copy From Basic button to copy the selected settings into the text box.
2. Double-click on any tag in the list to add it to the text box without typing.
3. You can use upper or lower case for operators. "Default.A AND Default.B" is equivalent to "Default.A and Default.B"
4. You can use the OR, AND, and NOT operators, plus parentheses () for grouping items, to produce some very complex expressions.
5. Advanced mode includes a syntax checker that flags errors, as shown in the example below whose typo - "Default.A andDefault.B" - is flagged by the "Unrecognized tag..." error message

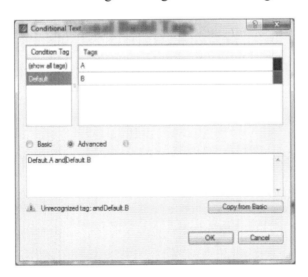

Three warnings about working in the Advanced mode or mixing Basic and Advanced mode.

1. Try to work in one mode. If you switch between modes, a change to your settings in Basic mode will overwrite the current settings in Advanced mode. This may be a big deal if you've created and overwrote a complicated expression.
2. Flare uses whichever mode is currently selected when you generate output. If you have different expressions in Basic and Advanced modes, you may get unexpected results in your output if you selected the wrong mode.
3. Document the logic and goals of your conditional work for the benefit of your successor on the project, or your own if you come back to the project after a long absence. Even the simplest of basic expressions can be confusing to someone who doesn't understand the project logic, and an Advanced expression can be even more confusing to someone who doesn't understand Boolean. That confusion can send your projects off-track.

Responsive Design and the "Un-Desktop"

Applies to version 10.

Consultants don't often make unequivocal statements but I'll make an exception for responsive design. I consider responsive design to be the most significant development in tech comm since the move from RTF to HTML in 1997.

What Is Responsive Design?

Responsive design uses elements of HTML5 and CSS3 to create *one* ("one" being the crucial word) online output that looks good on any device that exists today, and may exist tomorrow, no matter what the screen size and resolution.

What's the big deal, you ask? We can easily tailor our output to a small screen device by creating a new target for that device, using Flare's WebHelp Mobile target for example, and customizing its skin, stylesheet, and stylesheet medium for the new target.

But this means we now have two targets. And if another mobile device comes on the scene, with still different properties, we have to create yet another target for *that* device. And the next... At some point we'll run out of the resources needed to handle all the mobile devices to be supported. (In fact, the term "mobile" now applies to so many different devices with different screen sizes, resolutions, and other properties that the term "mobile" itself is almost meaningless. A better term might be "the un-desktop.")

Responsive design's benefit is that it doesn't require a separate target for each device. Instead, it lets you create one target that can automatically tailor itself to the device on which it runs.

There are many examples of responsive design on the web today. See "50 Best Responsive Website Design Examples of 2013" at http://socialdriver.com/2013/06/10/50-best-responsive-website-design-examples-of-2013/). One nice example is from the Children's Museum of Pittsburgh at https://pittsburghkids.org/ . Here's the site at full-screen.

Here it is at tablet size. (To simulate this, just shrink your browser window).

Note that some menu items are subsumed into the "More" menu item. Clicking "More" reveals the hidden items, as shown below.

Also notice the number and size of the small images along the bottom of the screen.

Reducing the image further, to a smaller tablet, produces this.

The four small images at the bottom have changed to two larger ones. Scrolling down reveals the other two images, also larger.

And here it is on a phone-sized screen, again simulated by shrinking the browser window.

The menu now shows what the museum considers to be the essentials – Visit Us, Call Us, and Find Us. All the other items are now subsumed into the Menu option at the upper right.

Again, you're not seeing multiple outputs, each formatted for different screen sizes. You're seeing one output that automatically formats itself based on the device screen size, resolution, or other properties.

The idea of responsive design is fairly new, arising from a 2010 article by Ethan Marcotte entitled "Responsive Web Design" at http://alistapart.com/article/responsive-web-design. (Read it if only for the rare opportunity to see an idea being born.)

As useful as responsive design appeared to be, its use within tech comm was limited by two factors in 2010, minimal involvement by tech comm with mobile devices and the need for familiarity with relative style units, fluid grids, and CSS3 media queries. But both of these factors are changing.

But first, if you're not familiar with relative style units, fluid grids, and media queries, here's a brief overview.

Relative Formatting

We typically specify text size in points - 72 pts = 1 inch. This is a familiar size unit from hard copy, but it's less effective online because it's "fixed" and doesn't scale in browsers. The alternative is "relative" units that can scale in different browsers and on different devices. Commonly used units today are % and em. (See the W3C discussion at http://www.w3.org/Style/Examples/007/units.en.html#font-size.)

Using relative formatting lets developers create content that can resize relative to some other unit. As a simplified example, the % is relative to the size of the default paragraph style in a browser. If normal is 100%, setting h1 to 160% makes h1 60% larger than the default paragraph style, with the effective size varying by browser. If browser A's default paragraph style equates to 10 pt, then a 160% h1 equates to 16 pt. If browser B's default paragraph style equates to 12 pt, then a 160% h1 equates to 19.2 pt. This lets the content adapt automatically to the device on which it's displayed. This relativity applies to other content elements too. For example, we can express a graphic's size as a percentage rather than a fixed size. So setting a graphic's width to 50% lets it change automatically depending on the screen space. The same holds true for tables and other elements.

Fluid Grids

A fluid grid is a layout that can change in response to changing screen size. For example, you might start with a grid that looks like this:

But changes to this as the screen gets narrower:

We don't see the grids behind the museum site but we do see its effect in how the layout changes. See http://www.1stwebdesigner.com/tutorials/fluid-grids-in-responsive-design/ for a good overview.

Media Queries

Media queries test for certain device properties and apply different styles based on the result. A media query might look like this:

```
@media screen and (min-width: 320px) {

}
```

This tests whether the device is a screen (a programmatically testable property) and whether its width is 320x or more. If a device meets these criteria, certain CSS settings take effect. This additional query:

```
@media screen and (min-width: 800px) {

}
```

This query then tests to see if the width exceeds 800px. If so, different CSS settings take effect. Each set of settings might reformat the screen or show or hide different elements, as seen in the museum site. The 320px and 800px figures are "breakpoints" and are the property at which the new CSS settings take effect.

As mobile devices become increasingly common, tech comm will have to get involved with them if only to not cede this niche to IT. And the need for code skills declined in the tech comm world starting in late 2013 when our HATs (help authoring tools) began to support it. Which brings us to Flare's support for responsive design, added in version 10 released in early 2014.

Responsive Design in Flare

Responsive design in Flare 10 is turned on and controlled through the HTML5 skin editor. (You *must* use HTML5 to get responsive output.)

Turn it on by selecting the Enable Responsive Output option in the Responsive Output Settings group at the bottom of the Setup tab on the HTML5 Skin Editor, shown below.

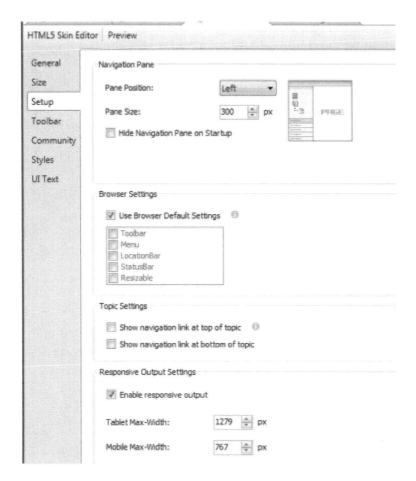

The Tablet Max-Width and Mobile Max-Width settings at the bottom are the "breakpoints," the screen sizes at which the screen layout will automatically change in response to media queries Flare adds.

The next step is to define what the screen should look like at each breakpoint. You do that using the Styles tab on the HTML5 Skin Editor, shown below.

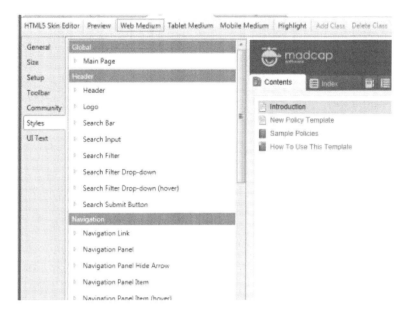

At the top are the three "mediums" labelled Web Medium, Tablet Medium, and Mobile Medium. Conceptually they're the same as mediums you set up and define in the Stylesheet Editor but are on the HTML5 Skin Editor instead. (A common mistake is to look for the responsive design mediums on the Stylesheet Editor.)

Below the mediums is the list of screen elements you can modify. They're collapsed in the image above. The image below shows one opened to illustrate some of the options available.

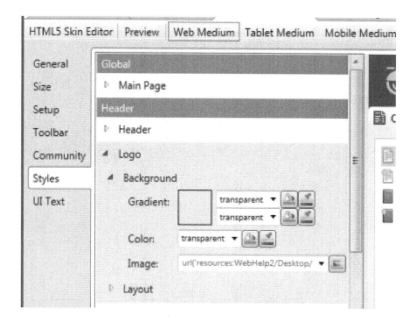

Any settings changes you make appear in the preview area to the right of the style options.

The idea is that you'd specify your settings for the Web Medium, which is big-screen output. Then specify different settings for the Tablet Medium and again for the Mobile Medium.

So the overall process is to:

1. Set the breakpoint values. You can use MadCap's defaults or modify them as needed.
2. Set the style settings for the three mediums.
3. Preview. You can preview the breakpoints by simply changing the size of your browser window, simulating the sizes of the actual mobile device screens.

4. Repeat steps 2 and 3 until you're satisfied with the settings for each medium.

Here's the result, using the Flare defaults. First, big-screen size.

Then reduced to a tablet size.

Notice that the Contents and Index panes are gone, subsumed in the slide-out icon in the upper left corner of the screen, and the MadCap logo moved from the left to the center.

Then reduced to smartphone size.

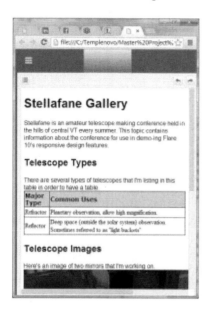

The only change here is the blanking out of the centered MadCap logo, just to show an effect at the smartphone-sized breakpoint.

Notice that there also a problem with the image. It has a fixed width that didn't resize when the window shrank and thus adds a horizontal scroll bar. This will be a problem when retrofitting legacy projects for responsive design.

Summary of Responsive Design

Just like the move to online content eliminated the constraints of paper, moving to responsive design eliminates the constraints of traditional PC screens. It opens new opportunities for technical communicators by expanding the universe of devices to which we can publish our outputs. This is why I consider it to be one of the most significant changes in technical communication in years.

Responsive design won't be widely adopted within technical communication overnight. It took years before online help became as significant a force as it is today. Similarly, it took years before HTML and XML became the dominant standards they are today. Implementation in legacy projects is likely to require the cleanup of a lot of local formatting, adoption of platform-agnostic content standards (such as switching from SWF to HTML5 for movies), and the adoption of new standards for writing content. (When the same content might appear on a PC and a smartphone, do we tell users to "click the button" or "tap the button"?)

Few of my training and consulting clients need responsive design yet, but everyone is aware of the explosion of new devices and the prospect of having to support them. Responsive output will help us do that.

Equation Editor

Applies to versions 8, 9, and 10.

One of the least-known features in Flare is the equation editor, the Equation option in the Symbols group on the Insert ribbon. In all my years working with Flare, only one person has ever even asked about it. But for a small group of Flare users, the equation editor is a blessing.

The equation editor is used by authors who write content that contains "real" scientific and engineering equations like this

$$h = \frac{M_u A_r(e) c_0 \alpha^2}{R_\infty} \frac{\sqrt{2} d_{220}^3}{V_m(\text{Si})}.$$

(From Wikipedia (http://en.wikipedia.org/wiki/Planck_constant) if you're curious - "The X-ray crystal density method is primarily a method for determining the Avogadro constant NA but as the Avogadro constant is related to the Planck constant it also determines a value for h." - h being Planck's constant. I'll stop there.)

In the past, and often still today, people who document such equations create them with tools like MATLAB from Mathworks (http://www.mathworks.com/) or Mathcad from PTC (http://www.ptc.com/product/mathcad/). But after creating the formulas, the authors have to take screen shots of them and insert the screen shots into the help topic. This is tedious if done once. It's far worse if you create a set of equations that build off previous equations, capture each one as a graphic, and insert the graphics only to find that you made a mistake in a previous equation and have to redo, recapture, and reinsert all the equations after the incorrect one.

To prevent this, the W3C created MathML (Mathematics Markup Language) in 1998 as an instance of XML. (See http://www.w3.org/Math/.) Today, MathML is part of HTML5 and thus widely available.

MathML lets authors create real equations in XML code while hiding the code, much like Flare lets you create topics in XML code while hiding the code. This eliminates the screen-capture-and-paste and thus speeds up the process.

For example, here's an equation that I produced to recreate the Planck's constant equation at http://www.colorado.edu/physics/2000/quantumzone/photo electric2.html

$$h = 6.626x10^{-34} J \bullet s$$

This equation is simple compared to the X-ray crystal density equation, simple enough that you could create it as text. But by creating it as XML, you can manipulate the code later without having to recreate and recapture the equation. Here's the underlying code:

```
<math>
  <mstyle mathvariant='italic'>
   |<mrow>
     <mi></mi>
     <mtext>h</mtext>
     <mo>=</mo>
     <mn>6.626</mn>
     <mo>&InvisibleTimes;</mo>
     <mi>x</mi>
     <mo>&InvisibleTimes;</mo>
     <mtext> </mtext>
     <msup>
```

You could also create this by hand if you were familiar with MathML code. Better to use the equation editor, shown below for the $h=...$ Planck's constant equation formula.

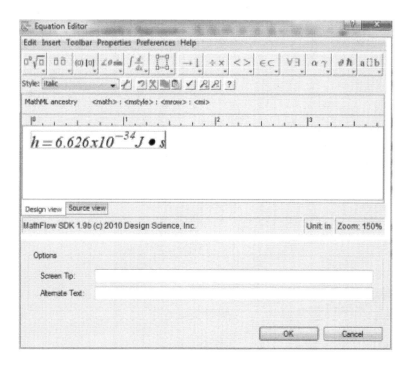

You can also select from one of the predefined option groups on the toolbar, as shown below:

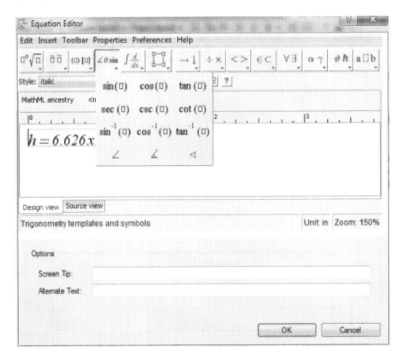

The lets you insert standard formula elements by simply clicking on them.

In summary, the equation editor is a visual and relatively simple way to create almost any equation imaginable.

Index

%

% unit of measure, 77

1

1st Heading and Title options, 46

A

Absolute units of measure for styles, 76

Adobe Integrated Runtime, 150

Advanced view, Stylesheet editor, 98

AIR, 150

Apps

    hybrid, 43, 189

    native, 43, 188

    web, 43, 188

Auto-generate print proxies in Flare 10, 118, 124

Auto-Reimport option, 139

Avoid Creating Empty Topics option, 135

B

Blocked content, turning off, 27

Breadcrumb trail, in master page, 65

Breakpoints, 214

Build tags, 195

C

Character styles on Styles pane, 104

Clear options, 15

Conditional build tags, 195

Conditionality logic, 197

Context sensitive help

open topic with navigation option, 145

overview, 142

Continuation paragraph styles for numbered lists, 113

Cross-Reference Format dialog box, 87

Cross-references

overview, 80

page number format for print output, 85

updating, 88

CSH, 142

open topic with navigation option, 145

CSS

apply one or more to a project, 160

mediums, 89

CSS3 media queries, 212

D

Dialog box

Insert Toggler, 62

Manage Named Elements, 61

Template Manager, 55

Doctype

overview, 25

quirks mode, 25

strict/standards mode, 25

Don't preserve MS Word Styles option, 129

Dropdown link conversion for print output, 172

E

ebooks, 189

eHelp, 41

Em unit of measure, 77

ePub

for mobile output, 41, 188

overview, 189

Equation Editor, 220

Ethan Marcotte - Responsive Web Design article, 209

Ex unit of measure, 77

Expanding link conversion for print output, 172

Expert space, 42

F

First Heading and Title options, 46

Flare Project Import, 156

Float, 10

assigning the sub-class to a graphic, 18

clear options, 15

float options, 14

issues and inconsistencies, 20

used through img style, 16

used through inline formatting, 11

used through sub-class of img style, 16

vertical alignment options, 16

Float options, 14

Fluid grids, 211

G

Glossary, 174

add to print output, 118

text vs. linked definitions, 182

Glossary definitions

text vs. linked, 182

Glossary tab

options for converting glossary term presentation, 174

Graphic float, 10

Graphic positioning, 10

Green marker box width, 127

Grids, fluid, 211

H

HTML 5

and content strategy, 41

and public-facing content, 41

and regaining the expert space, 42

and WebHelp, 41

benefits, 41

for mobile output, 41, 188

hybrid mobile apps

overview, 43

overview, 41

Hybrid mobile apps

and HTML 5, 43

overview, 43, 189

Hyperlinks vs cross-references, 80

I

Index

add to print output, 118

entry marker box width, 127

Insert Toggler dialog box, 62

L

Linked vs. unlinked TOC headings, 71

List styles

how to apply, 109

on the Styles pane, 109

Lists, numbered, 113

Local formatting and the Styles pane, 105

Logic of conditionality, 197

M

Manage Named Elements dialog box, 61

Mapping styles, 129

Marcotte, Ethan - Responsive Web Design article, 209

Mark of the Web, 27

Master page, 64

and topic-type templates, 67

in Flare help, 65

using multiple in one project, 66

Master page vs. page layout, 64

Master project, 156

Mathematics Markup Language, 220

MathML, 220

Media queries, 212

Mediums, 89

create new, 94

delete, 96

pre-defined types, 91

Mediums, for responsive design, 215

mobi, 190

Mobile apps

  and HTML 5, 43

  hybrid, 43

  native, 43

  web, 43

Mobile outputs, 41, 188

MOTW, 27

N

Naming content elements, 61

Native apps, 43, 188

Numbered lists

unnumbered paragraphs, 113

O

Open topic with navigation option, 145

P

Page layout vs. master page, 64

Page layouts

  overview, 67

  Page Setup in Word, 67

  setting properties for print outputs, 67

Page number format for print output, 85

Paragraph styles on the Styles pane, 104

Percentage

  unit of measure, 77

Points

unit of measure, 76

Popup link conversion for print output, 172

Popups

topic vs. text style, 163

Positioning graphics, 10

Preserve MS Word Styles option, 129

Print output

add a glossary, 118

add a TOC, 118

add an index, 118

and dropdown link conversion, 172

and expanding link conversion, 172

and popup link conversion, 172

and toggler link conversion, 172

page number format in cross-references, 85

page number format in xrefs, 85

Print proxies

auto-generate in Flare 10, 118, 124

Pseudo code view, 29

Q

Quirks mode, 25

R

Relative formatting, 210

Relative units of measure for styles, 76

Responsive design, 205

examples, 206

Responsive design mediums, 215

Responsive design, breakpoints, 214

RoboHelp, 41

S

Show Tags icon, 29, 127

Simplified view, Stylesheet editor, 98

Slideshows, 166

Source styles options in Word import, 129

Split Long Topics option, 132

Strict/standards mode, 25

Style mapping, 129

Styles

    absolute units of measure, 76

    relative units of measure, 76

Styles pane

and local formatting, 105

character styles, 104

paragraph styles, 104

Styles pane in Flare vs. other help authoring tools, 103

Styles, how to apply list styles, 109

Stylesheet editor

    advanced view, 98

    changing the view, 98

    show alphabetical list, 100

    show assorted relevant properties, 100

    show property groups, 100

    show set (locally) properties, 100

    show set properties, 100

simplified view, 98

Stylesheet mediums, 89

T

Table of contents headings

linked vs. unlinked, 71

Template Manager, 54

Template Manager dialog box, 55

Templates

creating, 53

overview, 51

renaming, 56

topic

overview, 51

Text popups, 163

TOC

add to print output, 118

TOC headings

linked vs. unlinked, 71

Toggler

links, 57

vs. dropdown, 57

Toggler link conversion for print output, 172

Topic

1st Heading and Title options, 46

First Heading and Title options, 46

Topic popups, 163

Topic templates

creating, 53

overview, 51

U

Unbind, 79

Un-desktop, 205

Units of measure

%, 77

em, 77

ex, 77

points, 76

Unnumbered paragraph styles for numbered lists, 113

Update

cross-reference, 88

xref, 88

V

Vertical alignment options, 16

W

Web apps, 43, 188

WebHelp AIR, 150

WebHelp for mobile output, 41, 188

WebHelp Mobile for mobile output, 41, 188

Width

green marker box, 127

index entry marker box, 127

Word import

Auto-Reimport option, 139

Avoid Creating Empty Topics option, 135

Source Styles option, 129

Split Long Topics option, 132

X

XHTML, working
directly in, 31, 38

Xref

overview, 80

page number format
for print output, 85

updating, 88

Made in the USA
San Bernardino, CA
13 March 2015